# AFRICA MUST UNITE

"This book is for every African man and woman it will make you proud of being African".

## BY VINCENT HAPPY MNISI

# CONTENTS

## PROLOGUE

This book outlines and clarifies the common need, and reasons for the unification of Africa. It looks at the Historical development from the 18th century, the scrambling for Africa, which led to the invasion by the European Imperialist forces that led to the colonial era from 1870. The main era of imperialism and colonialism was from 1870 to 1994. It highlights each countries liberation struggle against their colonial rulers. It outlines the different liberation movements their leaders and activities. and how each took control off their different parts of Africa. It outlines there directions of the each countries Independence leadership from their colonial rulers and how they ruled. It also highlights the coups and the internal political activities in each country. It gives guidance to the unification, a proposed structure of Democratic governance of each country and the unified Africa.

It is time to eradicate our legacy of internal tribal fighting and squabbling, it is time to set up democratic governance in each country answerable to a Central Government headed initially by an appointed President, who will be appointed from the democratically elected Presidents of each African Country. The African Presidency term of Two years will then rotate in alphabetical order to the different African Countries.

## THE REASONS

The main reason for the unification of Africa is purely social and economically driven. A united Gross Domestic Product (GDP) will enable Africa to form one currency which will enable the African currency to compete against the US dollar and the EURO in the world markets. The United Countries of Africa (UCA) has been in its infant stage for far to long in its current form as the Organisation of African Unity (OAU). This is due to the post colonial hangovers and influences from the former colonial rulers whom still have a vast influence on the economic development of each country. Even though all African countries have gained their independence from their imperialist colonial rulers, we are still heavily dependent upon their governmental systems; aid; educational; industrial and commercial trade links. Most countries are still being raped of their natural resources through the funding of rebel movements by their former colonial rulers which in turn causes distraction within the country as their continue to plunder our natural minerals right under our nose.

Africa should unite for the sake of the next generation to grow up in a liberated society which will enable them proposer in all their endeavours and for the sake of our history. We Africans owe it our ancestors; ourselves; our children and their children to put in place a Social Service Structure which will enable, to assist and inspire the next generation to develop without any hindrance. We Africans have a rich history of togetherness, of royal times, of our liberation leaders and their movements. We all need to read it to understand the past which will enable us determine our future. This book is for the Black race of the world because I believe in the saying that "if you are a black man no matter to where you were born you are an African" (Bob Marley). The key to self determination is Education.

## AFRICAN PARTITION

The African Partition is the division of the continent of Africa into colonial territories, which occurred in the last three decades of the 19<sup>th</sup> century. Europeans had traded with Africa for several centuries, using a series of coastal settlements. In the course of the 19<sup>th</sup> century, in the Europeans efforts of abolishing the slave trade, missionary endeavours and the optimistic views of African riches helped to encourage colonial ambitions. The countries involved in the partition were Britain; France; Germany; Portugal; Italy and Dutch Boers in South Africa in 1870. Only Liberia and Ethiopia remained independent when the French and the Italians completed the partition of North Africa in the years before the First World War. At the end of the Second World War, a repartitioning occurred with the confiscation of the German and Italian territories. All African countries have since achieved their independence in or after the 1960's the Organisation of African Unity (OAU) pledged itself to maintenance of the existing boundaries which were drawn by the imperialist during the partition. Imperialism explained is the extension of the power of a state through the acquisition, normally by force, of other territories which are then subject to rule by the imperial power. Many suggest that the motivation behind imperialism is economic, through the exploitation of cheap labour and resources and the opening up of new markets. Another explanation suggest that non economic factors may be involved which may included the motivation of nationalism, racism and the pursuit of international power. The main era of imperialism was between the 1880's to 1914 when European countries sought to gain territories in Africa and Asia. Imperialism in its past form of the European Empires has disappeared but the term is now often applied to any attempt by developed countries that interfere in underdeveloped countries. There is also an in the idea of neo-colonialism where certain countries are subjected by the economic power of developed countries, rather than direct rule we find cases of Indirect rule occurring. Indirect rule is the form of colonial rule which is especially characterised by the British rule in Africa during the inter-World Wars years. In general terms it also involved the use of existing political structures, Leaders, and local organs of authority. Thus meaning local political elites enjoyed considerable autonomy, although they still had to keep in accordance to the interest of the colonial power. Indirect rule was adopted on the grounds of its cheapness and to allow for the independent cultural development. It was increasingly criticized for it failure to introduce a modernizing role into the colonial administration. It was gradually given up after 1945.

The French and the British had the largest colonial empire; they established a system of dependency of the Colony whose economic and political administration served primarily not to it own needs but that of the colonial power. This system made it difficult for colonies to develop on their own terms and into their own direction. This situation has prevailed even after the granting of Independence, African countries have become the dependent countries of the under-developed Third world. The imperial conferences were a series of conferences at which representatives of the British colonies and dominions discussed matters of common imperial concerns usually held in London. The first colonial conference was held in 1887 and was followed by others in 1894; 1887; 1902; 1907; and 1911. They were followed by other conferences mainly concerned with the constitutional changes; defence; communications and economic matters in 1921; 1923; 1926; 1930 and 1937. After World War II they were replaced by the Conferences of the Common-Wealth Heads of government of the British Empire which later became known as The Commonwealth Of Nations.

## INTRODUCTION

This book is a comprehensive coverage of an A to Z of Africa's vast historic royal kingdoms in part one, it portrays an A to Z coverage of the key events in Africa in part two; and an A to Z of the people whom made African history through their liberation nationalist movements and on how they ruled in part three. It highlights the coups and counter coups, the military leaderships, the dictatorships and lately democratic movements and their leaders within each African country. In part four it gives guidance to the formation of the United Countries of Africa 'UCA'.

## PART ONE: AFRICAN ROYAL PAST AND PRESENT

- ➢ Abbas I(1813-54) Khedive of Egypt (1848/54): The grandson of the great Muhammad Ali, he took on an active part in his grandfather's Syrian War, but later did much to undo the progress made under him for example by blocking the construction of the Suez Canal.

- ➢ Abbas II (1874-1943) Khedive of Egypt (1892-1914): He succeeded his father Twefik Pasha and he attempted to rule independently of the British Empire. At the break of the First World War in 1914 he sided with Turkey and was deposed when the British made Egypt a protectorate.

- ➢ Ahomse I (Nebpehtire) (c1570/1546ʙ c): King of Egypt. He was the dynasty of Thebes, who drove the Hykos from Egypt. He became the first pharaoh of the 18ᵗʰ Dynasty and established the New Kingdom the period of the Egyptian Empire.

- ➢ Ahomse II (Khnumibre) (570/1546ʙ c): King of Egypt. Acceded to the throne following the defeat of his predecessor, Apries. Ahmose II relied on the Greek support during his long, peaceful reign. It was during the time that a Greek trading emporium was founded at Naukratis in the Nile Delta; by such a balancing of native Egyptian and Greek aspirations, the prosperity of Egypt was promoted.

- ➢ Ashanti (Asante): A Kwa-speaking people of Southern Ghana which is adjacent to areas of Togo and Ivory Coast. They formed a confederacy of chiefdoms, founded by the ruler Osei Tutu in the late 17ᵗʰ century. Their paramount Kingdom was established at Kumasi and their Golden Stool was their symbol of Ashanti Unity. The independent Ashanti state was at the height of its powers in the early 19ᵗʰ century by becoming a major threat to the British trade on the coast. They were eventually defeated in 1873 by a force under Sir Garnet Wolseley. The state was annexed by the British in 1902 after a further campaign in which the Golden Stool was seized and taken to London where it still is today. The Ashanti people have maintained their traditional culture and religion which still flourishes and is signified by their rich ceremonial rituals and their internationally acclaimed work of art.

➢ Askiya: The dynastic title of the rulers of Songhai, founded by Sunni Ali (1464/92) out of the disintegrating empire of Mali in Western Africa. The first Askiya, Muhammad Toure (died 1528) deposed Sunni Ali's successor in the 15th century and extended the empire into Eastern Mali and the Upper Volta Basin. He also re-established Timbuktu as a centre of Islamic faith and learning. He was deposed by his son in 1528 and the Songhai went into decline. The Empire dissolved altogether in 1591, when it was in invaded by the Moroccan army. The descendants of the Songhai Askiyas still continued to fight against their Moroccan rulers into the 17th century.

➢ Benin Kingdom: A powerful kingdom of South Nigeria rain forest founded in the 13th century which survived until the 19th century. The Dynastic title of the rulers was OBA. The Benin kingdom reached their imperial apogee under Ewuare the Great (1440/73). The Portuguese turned to the Benin Kingdom to source cloth, beads and slaves in the 15th and 16th century. It became one of the most prosperous kingdoms in Africa. The Benin Kingdom was conquered by the British in 1897, and in 1975 the name was adopted by the former French colony of Dahomey-kingdom of the West African Kingdom based in its capital Abomey. Which in the late 17th century and early 18th extended its authority from the coast to the interior, to the west of the Yoruba devastated Dahomey, but when the Oyo Empire collapsed in the early 19th century, Dahomey regained its power. It became famous for its trade in palm oil and slaves. It was heavily influenced by the neighbouring Yoruba tribe. Their state was annexed by the French in 1883, and it regained its independence renaming itself to Benin in 1960.

➢ Bunyoro Kingdom: One of the Kingdom of Uganda occupying territories in the north of Buganda. It was formerly the most powerful of these states, originally known as Kitara, before it was colonized by the Nilotic Bito. It declined in influence when Buganda rose in the 17th century. Buganda being one of the states of Uganda on the north-west shore of Lake Victoria. It began to expand in the 17th century and was very powerful by the 19th century. It was involved in trade in ivory and other commodities with the Nyamwezi in the 18th century. The Nyamwezi were people of the highlands of the north-central Tanzania, south of Lake Victoria. In the 18th century they created a trading network between the East African coast and some of the states of Uganda.

Later they extended their commercial influence to the Kazembe Kingdom in Zambia. These coastal Swahili speaking people were in touch with Europeans in the 19th century particularly during the reign of their Chief Marimbo.

➢ Changamire: The dynastic title of the rulers of Southern Zimbabwe from 1480 until the mid 17th century. In 1480 a vassal-ruler of the changa people took advantage of the weakness of the empire of the Monomotapa to declare himself an independent Amir (ChangaAmir). During the 17th century the Changamire also conquered most of Northern Zimbabwe (Mutapa) and formed a powerful barrier to the incursions of the Portuguese traders, eager to obtain access to the substantial gold-mining industry there. They were colonialised by the British in scramble for Africa.

➢ Denkyira: A state developed in the mid-17th century by one of the princes of the Akan people in the Western Gold Coast. Its power was based on gold and trade with Europeans on the Coast. However, it ruler never developed an effective imperial administration and it was weakened and eventually destroyed by competition and conflict with its eastern neighbour, the Akwamu state in the early 18th century. Akwamu in its turn was defeated in the 1730's and 1740's.

➢ Dingane (DIED 1843): king of the Zulu (1828/40). He was the successor to Shaka, he ruled at a time of increasing white penetration of the Natal. He had developed good relations with the white traders at Port Natal but became alarmed to land concessions by whites in North Natal. In February 1838 Piet Retief one of the leaders of the Boer Voortrekkers secured a grant of land, but he and his party were murdered on Dingane's orders on the same day. Retief was avenged at the Battle of Blood River, when Andries Pretourius defeated Dingane. Dingane was subsequently overthrown by his brother Mpande (1840/72), Dingane fled to Swaziland where he was killed.

➢ Dingiswayo (DIED 1818): Chief of the Mthethwa people, one of the northern Zulu Nguni tribe's people. Dingiswayo is credited for laying the foundation of the Zulu Kingdom state, which was later developed by Shaka in the 1820's. Dingiswayo ruled in the 1790's he set about a more centralised system among the northern Nguni tribe as a result of developing trade with Delagoa Bay or due to ecological problems in the region caused by a combination of rising population and severe drought. Dinginswayo then began the military revolution in particularly the development of age regiment; he also abolished the traditional ceremonies of circumcision. He was killed in 1818 following conflict with the rival Ndwandwe group. He was succeeded by Shaka Zulu.

➤ Djoser (Neterikhet) (c2700B.C): King of Egypt, he was the first king of the 3rd Dynasty at the beginning of the Egyptian Old Kingdom. The outstanding monument of his reign was the step Pyramid at Sakkara, the earliest free standing stone structure to be built, rising in six stages to a height of 204 feet. It formed part of a complex of buildings such as imitation shrines connected to the magical celebration of the seed-festival or jubilee of the dead king. The architect responsible for the monument was Emote who was later indentified with Asclepies by the Greeks. The relief and architectural features, together with a masterly seated statue of Djoser, demonstrates the technical skills reached at his early stage of the Old Kingdom.

➤ Farouk I (1920-65): The last king of Egypt (1936-52), was born in Cairo. He was educated in England and studied at the Royal Military Academy Woolwich. After World War II he turned increasingly to life of pleasure. The defeat of Egypt by Israel (1948) and the continuing British occupation led to increasing unrest and General Neguib's coup in 1952 forced his abdication and exile. In 1959 he became a citizen of Monaco. He later died in Rome in 1965.

➤ Fuad I (1868-1936): King of Egypt (1922/36). The son of Khedive Ismail Pasha, he was Sultan of Egypt from 1917, and became king when the British protectorate was ended. His position in Egypt was not helped by the fact that his father had been responsible for the sale of the Suez share to the British at a farcically low price. His brother had failed to rule before him which had led to the British Occupation of 1883. The Egyptian nationalist of the Wadf despised his dispensation, and his acquisitions. His flaunting off his conspicuous wealth coupled with his corrupt entourage of hanger on, who provoked adverse comments. In his attempt to control partism he suspended the constitution in 1931, but was forced to restore it in 1935. He was succeeded by his son, Farouk I who became the last king of Egypt. He was born in 1920 in Cairo.

➤ Galawdewos (DIED) 1559): The Emperor of Ethiopia from 1540-59, with aid from the Portuguese he defeated the Muslims who under Ahmad Gran Ahmad Iban Ibrahim Al Ghazi had dominated Ethiopia in the early years of the 16th century. He strengthened the authority of the monarchy and reformed the cultural and religious institution of the empire towards the end his reign he was preoccupied with the migration of Galla tribesmen but despite various successes in the battle (1554-5) was unable to permanently stop their advances.

➤ Gaza Kingdoms: One of the Kingdoms established by the northern Nguni people of whom the Zulu are the most famous. After their dispersal in Southern Africa known as the Mfecane, due to the defeat of Zwide by Shaka in 1819. Zwide the Chief of the Ndwandwe killed Dingiswayo during their battle for power in the emerging Nguni state in 1817 thus enabling Shaka to take over the Mthethwa army and later forge the Zulu state which became one of the most celebrated of all African states in the 19th century. The Gaza state people became the migrant labourers of the golden mines of the Witwatersrand Transvaal now known as Gauteng.

➤ Ghana Kingdom: A kingdom of the western Sudan which may have its origins as early as the 5-6th century, but which certainly flourished in the 8-11century. It probably derived its name from the title of its king, and bears no geographical relationship to the modern state Ghana which lies further to the South and East. It was one of a series of states on the margin between the savannah and the desert which controlled the trade of the Sahara. Its Capital was sacked by Almoravids in the 10th century and it power broken, though it lingered on until the 13th Century. They are made up of the Berber Hamito-Semtic speaking people of Egypt; Algeria; Libya; Tunisia and Morocco.

➤ Haile Selassie I (Prince Ras Tafari Makonnen) (1892-1975): Emperor of Ethiopia 1930/6 and 1941/74. He led the revolution in 1916 against Lij Eyasu and became regent and heir to the throne, becoming Emperor in 1930. He set about westernising the institution of his country, but was driven out when the Italians occupied Ethiopia in 1935 and settled in England. Restored in 1941 by the British, he became a father figure of African nationalism and was central to the establishment of the Organisation of African Unity, whose headquarters were established in Addis Ababa. His authoritarian rule, however, built up centres of opposition both among the elite and among non Amharic people. He survived an attempted coup in 1971, but famine of 1973 led to economic crisis, industrial strikes and ultimately a mutiny in the army and he was deposed in 1974, he died a year later at an army headquarters.

➢ Hassan II (1929- ): The king of Morocco in 1961, he was educated in France. He served his father as head of the army while he was Crown Prince Hassan, on his accession as king in 1961 he appointed himself Prime Minister. He also suspended parliament and then established a royal dictatorship from 1965 after riots in Casablanca. Despite having constitutional reforms in 1970 and 1977 he retained supreme religious and political authority. His forces occupied Spanish (Western) Sahara in 1957. He mobilised a large army to check the incursion of Polisario guerrillas across his western Saharan Frontier from 1976 to 1988. Unrest in the larger towns led Hassan to appoint a coalition government of national unity under a civilian Prime Minister in 1984.

➢ Hatshepsut (Maatkare) c (1489-1469B.C): Queen of Egypt she ruled in the 18th Dynasty, she was the daughter of Thutmose I and consort of Thutmose II. On the latter's death, Thutmose III, his by a minor wife, succeeded to the throne, with Hatshepsut, his step-mother, a regent. Supported by a group of officials, Hatsheput soon had herself crowned King with full powers, regalia and titles. She was represented herself in male attire including an artificial beard. The young Thutmose her son was kept in the background. During her 20 year reign she built her mortuary temple at Deir el Bahri, erected Obelisks at Karnak and despatched trading expedition to Punt (modern Eritrea/Somalia).

➢ Horemheb (Djeserkheorure) (c1339) (1304B.C) : King of Egypt he was a solider, he was the Commander-In-Chief of Tutankhamun's forces, who prepared a tomb at Sakhara, the sculpture reliefs of which feature campaign in Syria, Palestine, and Nubia. There were attempts to revive Egyptian power in territories which had revolted in the reign of Akhenaten. The royal line became extinct on the death of Tutankhamun he was succeeded by Horemheb Djeserkheprure an army officer who became king at Thebes, rather than at Sakkara. His main achievement was to prepare the way for the Ramesside rulers of the following dynasty, issuing an edict suppressing corruption and fraud, re-organising district councils and reforming the army.

> JaJa of Opodo (1821-91): West African merchant prince, he was an ex-slave. He established a highly successful trading operation in the Niger Delta before the partition of Africa. He founded his kingdom in 1869, when he led many of the constituent houses of the Kingdom of Bonny to his new capital to command the palm oil trade. He shipped oil directly to Britain and resisted European encroachments upon his trade. However he aroused the enmity of other traders, of missionaries and of the British Consul. In 1885 without any authorization from London Consul Sir Harry Johnston deposed him which became a significant move in the development of total British command of the Niger Delta.

> John IV (1831-89): Emperor of Ethiopia (1868/89). He succeeded Emperor Theodore, who committed suicide after the Napier invasion of Ethiopia in 1867-8. Although John wielded even greater power in Ethiopia than his predecessor, his authority was threatened in the 1880's by the Italians in Eritrea. Ethiopia was also under threat from the Mahdist Forces from the South of Ethiopia. In 1882 John came terms with Menelike accepting him as his successor. He was killed in battle with the Mahdist in 1889.

> Kabaka Yekka: Literally meaning 'The King Alone' the kingdom of Buganda who had support form the neo-traditionalist movement in Buganda organised round allegiance to the Kabaka or King of Buganda in the 1960's. It disintegrated when the Kabaka was forced into exile in 1966.

> Kanem: West African Kingdom situated to the north-east of Lake Chad under the Sefuwa Dynasty which survived from the 10th century to the 19th century. The strength of Kanem was based on its position between the forest was based and the desert and it ability to trade salt and copper from the north with forest goods and cotton from the south. Kanem's power was replaced by that of Bornu in the 15th century.

> Kazemba: Kingdom of Central African Kingdom founded in the mid-18 century by one of the dynasties that were off shoots of the Lunda Empire situated in the Luapula Valley between Mwera and Katanga. It occupied a strategic position rich in resources of salt, iron and copper which attracted the Portuguese. However it was divided in the late 19th century between King Leopold of the Belgians and Cecil John Rhode's British South Africa Company (BSAC).

➤ Khafre Kingdom: Chephren (c2558/2532) B C King of Egypt he was the fourth king of the 4th Dynasty in the Old Kingdom, who constructed the second largest of the pyramid of Giza towering to a height of 4474 feet. The mortuary temple at the eastern base of the pyramid was connected by a causeway with a valley temple is a massive building of limestone faced inside and out with slabs of Aswan granite. In this temple there was found a magnificent diorite seated stature of Khafre, now in the Cairo Museum. One of over 20 similar sculptures in various stones which originally stood in the temple. It conveys the calm dignity of an absolute monarch. Another outstanding monument of the Kings reign is the great Sphinx.

➤ Khama (1833-1923): The king of the Ngwato one of the Tswana people occupying the north of modern Botswana (1875-1923). He was a successful modernising ruler, who avoided the direct conquest of his Kingdom by seeking an accommodation with Europeans. In the late 19th century Khama tried to protect his state from the Ndebele to the North and the Boers to the east by securing the protection of missionaries and the British Imperial rule. He first sought the protection of the Queen Victoria 1876, but a protectorate was not granted until 1885 and Imperial rule was not fully established until 1891. He succeeded in avoiding control by the British South African Company which had secured a charter to rule in Rhodesia (Zimbabwe). Khama had already become a Christian, insisting on the conversion of his entire people when he converted. He issued laws to reform African traditional customs such bride-price and initiation ceremonies, he then also banned the brewing of strong Liquor in his kingdom. He visited London in 1895 on the occasion of the centenary of the founding of the London Missionary Society.

➤ Khama, Sir Seretse (1921-80): Botswana's Chief and politician Educated at Fort Hare College and London, where he trained as a Lawyer. He was the heir to the Chieftainship/Kingdom of the Ngwato he inherited the title in 1963. He was banned by the colonial authorities from returning to Bechwanaland because he married a white woman when he was permitted to return as a private citizen in 1956, he founded the Bechunana Land Democratic Party. He won a seat to legceo in 1965 and became President of the Republic of Botswana from its independence in 1966 until his death in 1980. He was plagued by health problems, he nevertheless managed to steer Botswana with great skill along a

Democratic path in the shadow of South Africa during its Apartheid years.

➤ Khedive: An ancient Persian title acquired from the Ottoman Sultan by the effectively independent Viceroy Of Egypt. Ismail Pasha in 1867. It was used until Egypt became a British protectorate (1994).

➤ Khufu (Cheops) (c2589/2566B.C): The builder of the Great Pyramid of Giza and the second king of the 4th Dynasty. The pyramid rose to a height of 481 feet, covered 13.1 acres in area and was composed of 2 300 000 blocks of limestone, each averaging two and a half tons in weight. Surrounding the pyramid were rows of tombs for the royal family and the King officials Near by were a number of pits designed to hold boats connected to the solar cult or the transporting of the dead king in the after life. Two held dismantled wooden boats, one of which is now re-assembled and displayed in a museum on the south side of the pyramid.

➤ Kongo Kingdom: An African kingdom situated to the south of the River Congo which by the 15th century had a coastline of 150 miles and reached inland for 250 miles. It was already involved in trade of ivory, copper and slaves when The Portuguese arrived in the area in 1482. Some of its kings accepted Christianity, but it was disrupted by the stepping up of the slave trade, and it then declined during the 18th century when the Portuguese turned their attention southwards to now what is called Angola.

➤ Kush: An Independent Kingdom on the Nile which emerged from the Egyptian province of Nubia in the 11th century before Christ. In the 8th century before Christ, Kush conquered Egypt and established the 26th Dynasty which ruled until the Assyrian conquest in 666-671B.C. The Kush became Egyptianized, but after their withdrawal from Egypt in the 7th century Before Christ they moved to the more southern Capital of Meroe, where the were good supplies of iron ore and timber. It became an important centre of iron smelting and large slag heaps can still be seen there.

➤ Lobengula (1870/93): King of the Ndebele or Matabele people of Zimbabwe. After a two-year succession crisis he succeeds his father Mzilikazi to rule directly over Matabeleland. He frequently raided and established authority over many of the Chieftaincies of the Shona people in Mashonaland. During his reign many Europeans, prospectors, hunters, missionaries, traders and concession seekers reached his Kingdom from the South. He became embroiled in complex diplomatic negotiation and set out to protect his Kingdom with great astuteness. However Cecil John Rhodes succeeded in securing key concessions for mining and land alienation in Mashonaland which enabled him to secure a charter for his British South Africa Company and invaded Mashonaland in 1890. Lobengula attempted to maintain a peaceful co-existence with the white settlers, but was forced into war in 1893. The Ndebele were defeated and Lobengula died, possibly of small pox while fleeing north to the Zambezi (Zambia). He left a number of sons who were claimant to the throne of the Matabele people but the region was incorporated into Southern Rhodesia by Cecil John Rhodes. The Ndebele rose in revolt in 1896 and appointed Nyamanda as King; they also sued for peace later the same year. Their Chieftaincies Kingdom still survives to-date in the Ndebele tribe of Zimbabwe whose population was massacred in the Zanu PF Grugahundi genocide of Matabeland by a Shona Robert Mugabe's ZANU PF thugs who is the current dictator of Zimbabwe.

➤ Lozi (Barotse) state: A state formed by a cluster of Bantu-speaking agricultural and cattle-herding people of western Zambia, living in the flood plains of the upper Zambezi. It was penetrated by hunters, traders and missionaries in the late 19th century and under king Lewanika, peacefully accepted colonial rule. During the colonial period the state was known as Barotseland and was controlled by indirect rule, so that their kingship and distinctive institutions survived.

➤ Luba-Lunda kingdoms: A succession of African states occupying territory in what is now Zaire. They were powerful by the 17th century involved in slave trade and ivory trading with the Portuguese and later with Zanzibar. The Luba states were relatively unstable, but the Lunda Empire seems to have consolidated its power through trade. The central Lunda state did not survive the ending of the Angolan Slave trade in the 1840's and the other fell to European imperialism.

- Mali: Kingdom of Major medieval kingdom of the Western Sudan which flourished between the 13<sup>th</sup> century and 15<sup>th</sup> century and dominated by Muslim merchants. It was visited in 1352-3 by the Great Arab traveller and geographer Ibn Bttuta, who commented on its prosperity and Freedom from violence. It declined in the 15<sup>th</sup> century.

- Maravi Kingdom: An African kingdom which was situated north of the Zambezi and south of the Lake Malawi, which has given its name to the modern Malawi (Maravi). It had a loose Confederation of Chiefdoms under a titular head which occupied territory spanning land in Malawi, Zambia, and Mozambique. Its people were involved in long distance trade, and in the 17<sup>th</sup> century its power reached the Eastern African Coast but it was disrupted by the migration of the Ngoni in the early 19<sup>th</sup> Century.

- Menelik (1848-1913): Emperor of Ethiopia, the King of Shoa, he succeeded John IV, when he was killed in 1889 in the battle with the Mahdist in the Sudan. Menelik had conquered the Galla and Somali people adding the Ogaden to the Ethiopian state and he then cultivated the Europeans, particularly the Italians. He was probably the most powerful indigenous rulers in Africa, but he faced threats from a number of quarters. The Egyptian imperialism from the North, the Mahdist from the Sudan and the Italians in Eritrea and Somalia. He concluded the treaty of Wichale or Ucciadi with the Italians considered that it gave them a protectorate over Ethiopia and advanced into the interior to make good their claims. However, Menelik had equipped himself with supplies of modern armament; his army defeated the Italians at the Battle of Adowa in 1896, which became the greatest success of the African resistance against European imperialism in the Partition of Africa. Mussolini Later revenged the defeat at Adowa by invading Ethiopia again in 1935 during the reign of Haile Selassie I.

- Menkaure (Mycerinus)(c2532-2504B.C): king of Egypt, the fifth king of the 4<sup>th</sup> Dynasty, he was the builder of the third pyramid at Giza, forming with those of Khufu and Khafre the only surviving monument of the seven wonders of the world. At an original height of 218 feet, a much smaller building than either of its predecessors, it was partly cased in granite from Aswan. This material was brought down river from the Southern quarries in the contrast to the more easily obtained local limestone. They were a series of finely sculpted slate statues of the king accompanied by his Queen and various statues of goddesses which were recovered by the Harvard University-Boston Museum of Fine Arts excavation team. These were conducted between 1905 and 1927 at the Giza site, which included the valley building and mortuary temple connected with the pyramid, where the statues were found.

➢ Mentuhotpe II (Nebhepetre) (c2060/2010B.C): king of Egypt the king of the 11th Dynasty from Thebes, he reunified Egypt in c2040 B.C. following a period of its instability, and the inaugurated the Middle kingdom. He fostered a period of peace and prosperity, winning the loyalty and the support of local Princes in the provinces. There was a gradual return to fine craftsmanship in place of the careless, ungainly work of the preceding Intermediate period. Mentuhotpe's ruined mortuary temple at Deir al Bahri in the western Thebes he had a raised terrace approached by a ramp, supporting a Square building, either pyramidal or flat topped by porticos on two levels.

➢ Merenpath (Baenre) (c1224/1213B.C): King of Egypt, he was the thirteenth son of Ramesses II. In the fifth year of his reign the Egyptian repelled an invasion by Libyans and their allies, the people of the sea somewhere in the Delta. From his reign there exist the only Egyptian written record of the name (Israel) implying its recognition as an entity possibly some two generation following the Exodus from Egypt (c1275B.C)

➢ Middle Kingdom: In Ancient Egyptian history, the period c2040-1786 B.C covering the last 50 years of the 11th Dynasty to the end of the 12th Dynasty. The founders were the princes of Thebes whom extended their authority throughout Upper and Lower Egypt, reunifying the country with a central government control, in place of the disruption of the first Intermediate Period. Mines and quarries were again worked and trade renewed. Architecture and art regained their former high standards of design and crisp execution. In the 12th Dynasty, by strong government, the adoption of a co-regency to ensure the smooth transition from one ruler to another and the establishment of an almost feudal system to obtain support of the country into a stable, prosperous condition. The conquest of Lower Nubia was undertaken with the boundary set at the 2nd cataract on the Nile. Contacts were maintained with Western Asia, particularly the ports of Byblo's. The craftsmanship of the Middle Kingdom jewellers and goldsmith was unsurpassed in taste, beauty of design and technical skills. The strength of the Middle Kingdom administration is demonstration by its being officials in the succeeding 13th Dynasty in spite of the short and ever weaker rule of a number of petty kings.

➤ Mirambo (c1840-84): king of the Nyanwezi people, he was the most important warrior kings of the Nyanwezi people of Tanzania who became traders connecting the East African coast to the interior in the 19th century. Mirambo created military bands of followers called Ruga-Ruga who were influenced by the age regiment system of the Ngoni people, and by 1870's was able to control the Swahili traders conveying ivory and slaves to the coastal port.

➤ Moshesh (c1786-1870): King of the Southern Sotho people, he was founder of the state which has survived as the independent Lesotho, surrounded by South Africa. Moshesh was the son of a small chieftain who succeeded in the creating a congeries of people to protect themselves from the marauding Nguni people Flooding out of northern Natal in the Diaspora known as the Mfecane. From his stronghold at Thaba Bosia he was able to build his power and play off the rivalries of the Boer and British in the 1840's and 50's. He invited French Protestant missionaries to his Kingdom and although he was not a Baptized, he then adopted some customs to missionary demands. In turn he used the missionaries as his protectors and go between. In 1868, he persuaded the British to annex his Kingdom to avoid further encroachment and attacks from the Boers. After a brief period when Bosuto-land was administered from the Cape. Moshesh's state was transferred directly to the British in 1880.

➤ Moshoeshoe II Constantine Bereng Seciso (1938- ) King of Lesotho (1960-90). Educated at Roma College, Ampleforth and Corpus Christian College, Oxford. He was installed a Paramount Chief of the Basotho in 1960 and then proclaimed king when Lesotho became independent in 1966. His political involvement resulted in him being placed under house arrest twice. In 1970 he spent eight months in Exile in Holland. He returned on the understanding that he would behave a constitutional monarch. He remained King after the Military coup in January 1986, but was later exiled again in March 1990 to England. He was called back by Major General Lekhanya but he refused in the same year in

November 1990 his eldest son succeeded to the Throne as King Lestsie II.

➤ Muhammad Ali (c1769-1849): The Viceroy of Egypt 1805 to 1848. He was an Albanian military officer, he was sent to Egypt with a Turkish-Albanian force on the French invasion in 1798. After the French left, he supported the Egyptian ruler in their struggle with the Mamluks and became the Chief power in Egypt (1805). He formed a regular army, improved irrigation and also introduced elements of European civilization. He extended Egyptian territory, routing the Ottoman army at Koniya 1832, but the Quadruple alliance of 1840 compelled him to limit his ambitions to Egypt. In 1848 he became insane and was succeeded by his adopted son Ibrahim.

➤ Mutesa I (c1837-84): Long-reigning Kabkka/king of Buganda (1856-84) under his rule the power of the monarch and the extent of the kingdom on the northern shore of the Lake Victoria were greatly increased. Mutesa was fascinated by the Muslim Zanzibar traders who visited his court and was eager to supply him with modern firearms. His court developed Islamic practices, but Mutesa was also beset by Christians Europeans, in 1896 a religious persecution created Muslim martyrs. He invited both Catholic and Protestant missionaries to Buganda to try to balance them against each other and also encourage the restoration of indigenous religion. His successor Mwanga, inherited a religious powder keg.

➤ Mutesa II (1924-69): Kabaka or King of Buganda (1939/53 and 1955/66). Mutesa was educated in England and was an honorary captain is the Grenadier Guards. He succeeded as Kabaka during World War II and set about safeguarding the position of his kingdom within Uganda, even attempting to lead it to separate independence. At the centre of several controversies relating to the independence and post colonial politics of Uganda. Mutesa was exiled 1953-5 by the Governor Sir Andrew Cohen for opposing British plans for unitary decolonization. On Independence he was briefly President of Uganda with Milton Obote as his Prime Minister, but in 1966 Obote overthrew him in a coup. Mutesa escaped to London where he died.

➤ Mwata Yamvo (1600-mid 19th century): The Dynastic title of the paramount chiefs of the Lunda Empire of Central Africa. The empire expended steadily from its inception in c1600 so that by the mid 19th century as many as 36 great chiefs of the region were reputed to pay tribute to the Mwata Yamvo.

> Mwene Mutapa: The Dynastic title of the Kings of Northern Zimbabwe with whom Portuguese trader established close relations in the 16th century. Gatsi Rusere (d1622) appealed to the Portuguese for aid in suppressing a rebellion from his brother ceding in return for mineral wealth of the Kingdom to his brother in arms the King of Portugal. Towards the end of his reign relations with the Europeans deteriorated although the king received baptism on his death bed. His son Nyamdi Kaparide broke openly with the Portuguese and placed himself at the head of an uprising in 1631. He was defeated in the battle in 1633 and then replaced by the puppet-King Mavura (d 1652), after which the Dynasty survived only in Subordination to the Portuguese who had crossed over from Mozambique.

> Mzilikazi (c1790-1868): Chief of the Ndebele (c1820/68). He was head of the Ndebele of the Nguni groups which had clashed with Shaka during the 1820's. Mzilikazi led his peoples and finally settled in what is now the western Transvaal-Western Gauteng. The missionary Robert Moffat made contact with him and they established a close relationship. Mzilikazi came into conflict with the Boer Voortrekkers and was defeated by a Boer commando under Hendrik Portgieter in 1837 near the modern Pretoria. He and his people then moved northwards crossing the Limpopo River settling in what is now Bulawayo South Western Zimbabwe. There he established his power over the Shona people and succeeded in keeping whites at bay until his death.

> Narmer Menes (c 3100B.C): King of Egypt, he was the founder of the 1st Dynasty he is considered by some scholars to the king who accomplished the unification of Egypt c3100 B.C strong evidence for this exists in a ceremonial slate palatal is now in the Cairo Museum, which shows the King wearing the crown of Upper and Lower Egypt, symbolizing his claim to be the development at this early period of a method of writing, the hieroglyphic scripts. Memphis, the capital of Egypt was traditionally established by Narmer at the apex of the Nile Delta. Some authorities hold that the Menes of Manetho and Egyptian priest who wrote a history of Egypt during the Ptolemic Period, combine in a single character both Narmer and his successor Aba.

➢ Ndongo: A Kingdom to the south of the Congo at the mouth which the Portuguese first encountered in the late 15th century. Its ruler was known as Ngolo and gave his name to the present Angola. The Portuguese attempted to turn Ndonga into a Major slaving partner and also embroiled it in a major slaving partner and also embroiled it into war with the Kingdom of Kongo. A new Kingdom known as Matamba emerged from it's in the 16th century, but like its neighbours it was eventually subsumed within the Portuguese colony.

➢ Necho II (Wehemibre) (610/595ʙᴄ): King of Egypt he attempted to link the Nile with the Red Sea by means of a canal, but the understanding had to be abandoned. In commissioning Phoenician ships to circumnavigate Africa, however, the king had more success. After the fall of Nineveh to the Medes and Babylon's (612ʙᴄ) and the end of the Assyrian Emoire, Necho was the Chief opponent of Nabopolassar of Babylon. Referred to in the Old Testament as 'Pharaoh-Necho' the killing of Josiah of Judah at the Battle of Megiddo by the Egyptian king is mentioned in 2 Kings XXIII 29-30. Necho with a fleet was able to control the coast of Ohoenicia and in 606-605ʙᴄ He mounted attacks on the Babylon's on the Egyptians were defeated at Carchemish by Nebuchadhezzar son of Nabopolassar. In 601ʙᴄ the Babylonians marched against Egypt once more but were driven off and retreated to Babylon.

➢ Nectanebo II (360 343ʙᴄ) King of Egypt he came to the throne as result to a disastrous expedition, led by Teos the Persians in Phoenicia. The Greeks supported Nectanebo and following the defeat of Teos, who fled to Persia and exile, he returned to Egypt as the last native King. A considerable number of buildings, particularly in the Memphite area, owed their construction to him. In Persia meanwhile, Artaxerxes III Ochus was bringing order to shaky empire. Dealing first with revolt in Phoenicia and Palestine, by 343ʙᴄ he had attacked Egypt at Pelusium and two other points in the Delta; Nectanebo surrendered, the garrison having been promised fair treatment soon after other Delta towns surrendered and Nectanebo realising that further resistance was hopeless, he sett off to Nubia and vanished from history.

➢ Nefertiti (Neferenefruaten) (14ʙᴄ): Queen of Egypt, she was the consort of Amenhotpe IV (Akhenaten) and the mother of six daughters. Nefertiti was closely associated with the King as is evident from the painted reliefs in the Aten Temple at Karnak, where she figures prominently, and at El Amarna in Tomb scenes. The new realism in art is nowhere better shown than in the portrait head of the Queen now held in the Berlin Museum.

➢ Nyoro Kingdom: A Bantu-speaking agricultural people of western Uganda. The original feudal Kingdom of Bunyoro-Kitara was founded in the 14-15ᵗʰ century with a pastoralist ruling class (Hima) and farming peasants (Iru). It was the most destroyed by the British in the 1890's. The kingship was abolished by Idi Amin in 1966.

➢ Nzinga Queen of the Matamba (d1663). A royal princess of the Ndonga a small Kingdom adjoining the Portuguese colony of Angola, she fought to establish a Kingdom independent of the Portuguese, free from war and depredation of the slave trade. In 1623 she went personally to Angola to negotiate with the governor and was baptized a Christian as Dona Ana de Souza. She was eventually driven out of Ndongo by the Portuguese troops the following year, she created the new Kingdom of Matamba where she trained up military elites to resist the Portuguese and she allied her Kingdom with the Dutch following their capture of Luanda the Angolan Capital in 1641. Although she had abandoned Christianity she reconverted towards the end of her life, by which time Matamba had become a successful commercial kingdom largely through acting as a broker in the Portuguese slave trade.

➢ Oyo: kingdom of the dominant Yoruba (Nigeria) state of the 17ᵗʰ century and the 18ᵗʰ century. Both the Oyo Dynasty and those of the other kingdoms of the Yoruba were said to have been founded by decedents of the Ife and their people were notably town dwellers. The success of the Oyo was based on its cavalry, which extended the Kingdom South-Westward and also jostled from power with its neighbouring savannas states Borgu and Nupe. Its expansion was based on securing the salt trade and the trading routes to the coast associated with European slaving. In the 18ᵗʰ century it came into conflict with Dahomey and won the war of 1726-30. In the early 19ᵗʰ century, Oyo became a victim of the Jihads or Holy Wars of the period. Its northern territory became the Fulani emirate of Ilorin, and the state broke up into series of small states competing with each other in incessant rivalries and warfare.

➤ Pepi II (Phiops) (c2278/2184ʙ.c): King of Egypt according to the chronicle of the Egyptian kings drawn up by Manetho, an Egyptian king drawn up by Manetho an Egyptian priest of the Ptolemaic Period, Pepi came to the Throne when six years of age and lived to be a hundred. Some support for this is found in a papyrus known as the Turin Canon of the kings from the reign of Ramesses II which gives Pepi a reign of over 90 years. This very human reaction of the boy King are recounted in a letter sent to Hrkhuti, the Governor of Elephantine, on the latter's return from an expedition into Nubia, bringing a dancing dwarf as a gift to his royal master. Under Pepi's rule, foreign trade was carried on together with expeditions to the Turguoise mines in Sinai and the quarrying operation in the eastern desert.

➤ Ptolemy II; Ptolemy III; Ptolemy IV; Ptolemy V; Ptolemy VI: Egyptian Pharaohs (look up their history on the internet).

➤ Senusret II Khakeheperre (1979/1928ʙ.c): King of Egypt. One of the most vigorous rulers of the 12th Dynasty, he was the fourth king of that family. There are no records of his having tried to extend Egypt's foreign conquest. Instead quarries and economic and the agricultural improvement in Egypt. It was apparently Senusret II who began a scheme of land reclamation and flood control of the Nile waters in the Fayum.

➤ Senusret III (Khakaure) (c1878/1843ʙ.c): King of Egypt he was the fifth King of the 12th Dynasty =, he was a key figure in the Middle Kingdom. His reign was significant in two important respects. Firstly he intervened during the second half of his reign to deprive the monarch or provincial Governors of their status and privileges. The kings other achievement was the strength of Egypt's hold on Nubia campaigns were mounted in the eight tenth, sixteenth and nineteenth years of his reign to enforce Egyptian authority. An armed foray was also made into Palestine as far as the biblical Shechem. The Southern boundary was settled at Semma at the head of the Second Cataract, protected by a line of forts situated at strategic points.

➢ Seti (Men-maat-Re) ($c$1303/1290$_{B.C}$): King of Egypt he was the second king of the 19$^{th}$ Dynasty, Seti succeeded his elderly father, Ramesses I, who riled for only a very short period following the disruptive effects of the Amarma episode Seti restored Egypt's standing as a great power in Western Asia. Scenes carved on the walls of the temple of Amun at Karnak show campaigns waged tore-establish Egyptian influence in Palestine and Syria. The fourth of these operations was against the Libyans and which provided a foretaste of the trouble experienced by Ramesside Kingdom. In Egypt itself the effectiveness of the administration is shown by the amount building undertaken by Seti.

➢ Seyyid Said (1791-1856): Sultan of Oman and Zanzibar (1806-56). The greatest of the sultans of the Al-Busaid Dynasty he was a merchant prince who ruled in both the Arabian Peninsula and East Africa between 1806 and his death. He visited the East African Coast over which Oman had a vague suzerainty, dating from the 17$^{th}$ century in 1827-8. He recognised the potential of the Island of Zanzibar and Oemba; he encouraged members of his Omani aristocracy to found clove plantatations there. By 1840 he had moved his capital to Zanzibar making it the East African Coast. The USA opened trading relations and the British established a powerful consulate. On Said's death, the British arbitrated the succession dispute. Under the Canning Awards of 1862, the combined Sultanate of Oman and Zanzibar was divided between two of his sons.

➢ Shaka (1727-1828): King of the Zulu (1817/28). He was the most famous of the Zulu kings he built on the military achievement of his predecessor, Dingiswayo. He extended the Zulu state and contributed to the great dispersal of the Nguni speaking peoples into Southern Africa known as the Mfecane. Shaka was the illegitimate son of Sezangakona, the Chief of the small clan known as the Zulu, whom were conquered by Dingiswayo's Mthethwa tribe. When Dingiswayo was killed in battle with the rival Ndwandwe. Shaka's military genius enabled him to take over the Mthethwa army. In1819 his troops using the short stabbing Assegai spear and the encircling attack formation which he introduced. He defeated the Ndwandwe and welded together a considerable state in the Northern Natal. His rule became a by-word for ruthlessness although he maintained reasonably good relations with the Europeans traders settled at Port Natal. His victories sent shock waves to the Nguni people and it sent them scattering Natal, the Transvaal (Gauteng) and areas of central Africa and East Africa as far a North Lake Victoria.

➤ Sobbuza II (1899-1982): king of Swaziland. Educated at Lovedale College, he was installed as Paramount Chief or Ngwengama of the Swazi people in 1921. He was Head of State when Swaziland became independent in 1968. In 1973 he assumed full executive and legislative powers and introduced a new constitution in 1978 which re-established traditional authorities, rather than universal suffrage, as the basis of legitimate authority.

➤ Sneferu Neb-maat (c2613/2589BC): King of Egypt

➤ Yusuf bin Hassan (Jeronimo Chingula) (1526/31). Last Sheik of the Malindi Dynasty of Mombasa (Kenya). As a youth he studied under Portuguese Tutelage in Goa and was baptized a Christian as Don Jeromino Chingulia. Following his succession in 1526 he took up arms in 1531 against the Portuguese domination, he was driven out of Mombasa and direct Portuguese rule was established.

➤ Thutmose I (Akheperkare); Thutmose III Pharaohs of Egypt.

➤ Zwangendaba (d1845). King General in the Nwandwe army of the Northern Natal. After being defeated at the hands of Shaka the Great in 1819, he took his followers northwards and settled near Delagoa Bay in Portuguese Mozambique. In 1831 Zwangendaba moved onto attack the Shona in Great Zimbabwe, crossed the Zambezi River in 1835 and established military states in both the modern Malawi and Tanzania. These states in resisted the establishment of European rule in the Partition of Africa initially.

➤ Zwide (d 1819): Chief King of the Ndwande, he was head of one of the northern tribes of Northern Natal. The Ndwandwe and the Mthethwa under Dingiswayo was killed when attacked by Zwide in 1817, thus enabling Shaka to take over the Mthethwa army and forge the Zulu Empire State, which was one of the most celebrated of all African kingdoms states in the 19th century.

**PART TWO**: An A to Z of African events, political parties their leaders, events and people that have made African history what it is today.

> ➢ Adowa Battle (March 1896): A battle between Ethiopian forces under Emperor Menelik and the Italian forces in which the Italians were decisively defeated. In 1880 Italy had become involved in the Scramble for Africa taking Eritrea 1884 and the Indian Ocean coast of Somalia 1890. The Italian defeat of Adowa was the worst reverse suffered by the Europeans in the Partition of Africa and ensured Ethiopian Independence for another 40 years. It was also probably the biggest factor in bringing down the second Crispin Ministry. Mussolini's invasion of 1935 was a conscious act of revenge to their lose at Adowa.

> ➢ African Development Bank: Established in 1963 in the same year as the Organisation of African Unity and is based in Abidjan. It began operation in 1966, its funds come from individual countries and multilateral sources and loans a made on preferential rates to African countries for development.

> ➢ African Lakes Company: A company founded in 1878, originally called the Livingstone Central Africa Company, to assist the Scottish Presbyterian missionaries in Nyasaland (Malawi). Its founders the two brothers Fred and John Moir placed steamers on the Lake Nyasa and became embroiled in campaigns against Muslim rivals. The under-capitalized company was poorly managed and it was bought out by Cecil Rhodes who in 1893 turned it into the African Lakes Trading Corporation. It remained a leading trading and retailing company throughout the period of colonial rule in Central Africa.

> ➢ The African National Congress (ANC): The South African nationalist organisation opposed to white minority rule in South Africa. It began in 1912 as the South African Native National Congress under the influence of M.K Ghandi, who organised passive resistance to white power. He led members of a growing black middle class; it steadily extended it support both into some urban black communities and also into liberal white quarters. Its central policy document The Freedom Charter was issued in 1956. It was a social democratic statement believing in non-racialism rather than the racial exclusivity of its rival Pan Africanist Congress (PAC). ANC was declared an unlawful organisation in April 1960; it then began its military wing (Umkonto We Sizwe) which

essentially followed a two-track policy of direct action within South Africa and diplomacy abroad. It was generally recognised as the dominant voice of black protest by the National Party in South Africa. Nelson Mandela, Walter Sisulu and many other political prisoners were Incasrated in the Reviona Trial of 1964 were their spent 27 years in prison on Robben Island before being released by President F.W De Klerk in February 1990 when the ANC and all other political parties were unbanned. F. W De Klerk instigated the CODESA Conference talks which led to the transition to a democratic South Africa the last African country to gain full independence in 1994.

➢ African National Council: A Zimbabwean political organisation founded in 1972 on the roots of the Zimbabwean African People Union (ZAPU) to express to the Pierce Commission black opposition to a proposed constitutional arrangement agreement agreed between Ian Smith and British Prime Minister Sir Alec Douglas-Home. Its leader was Bishop Abel Muzorewa who developed it into a political party. Its success in the late 70's depended upon the continued banning of its forerunners and its strength rapidly reduced after Independence in 1980.

➢ Afrikaner Bond: A society founded in 1880 as part of the political and cultural revival of the Boers in South Africa. It coined the slogan "Afrika voor de Afrikaners' it promoted the Dutch language and strict Calvinism. There were branches in the Cape, Orange Free State and Transvaal. At the Cape the Bond was prepared to form a political alliance with English-speaking South Africans, particularly supporting Cecil Rhodes, but elsewhere it became virulently anti-British. In 1918 a new body, The Afrikaner Broederbond emerged it was much more secretive becoming the driving force to more radical Afrikaner Nationalism in the 20th Century.

➢ Afrikaners an early term to describe the Europeans who had been born in the Dutch colony of the Cape and where therefore 'Africans', also known as the Boer (in Dutch farmer). During the 18th century they penetrated the interior of the Cape as pastoral farmers. After 1835 groups left the Cape and established independent republics in the interior which later coalesced into the Orange Free State. The Boer Wars of 1880-1881 and 1899-1902 these two wars were fought by the British and the Boers for the mastery of South Africa. The British had made several attempts to re-incorporate the Boers, who had left the Cape Colony in the Great

Trek, within the South African Confederation. The first Boer war ended with the defeat of the British at Majuba Hill and the signing of the Pretoria and London Convention 1881 and 1884. In 1896 the Jameson Raid was a clumsy private effort to achieve the same previous objective. The second Boer War can be divided into three phases the first being from October 1899 to January 1900 which cumulated in the series of the Boer successes which included the sieges of Ladysmith, Kimberly and Mafeking as well as victories at Stormberg, Modder River, Magersfontein, Colenso and Moderspruit. The second phase was from February to August of 1900 which was a British counter-offensive led by Lord Roberts which included the raising of the sieges, the British victory at Paardeberg and the capture of Pretoria. The third phase was from September 1900 to May 1902 which was a period of guerrilla warfare in which Herbert Kitchener 1st Earl attempted to prevent the Boer commando raids on isolated British units and lines of communications. The Boers effectively won the peace by the Vereeniging Peace of 1902 treaty which ended the Boer Wars. This treaty was signed at Pretoria; the Boers won three important concessions: First An amnesty for those who had risen in revolt within the Cape Colony. Secondly a promise that the British would deny the franchise to Africans until after the Boer republics were returned to a representative government and thirdly an additional financial support for reconstruction. The peace ensured that there would be significant change in the political relationship of white and blacks in South Africa from the foundation for the creation of Apartheid. Apartheid (Afrikaans 'Apartness') this policy introduced by the Boers in order to separate racial development in the Republic of South Africa, supported traditionally by the Nationalist Party and more recently by other right wing parties such as the AWB (Afrikaanse Weestand Beweging Resistance Movement) it was a Para-military group founded in 1973 by Eugene Terri' Blanche who led it was prepared to support its aims of preserving white control of South Africa by force. The ideology of Apartheid has several roots one of which the Boer concept of racial, cultural and religious separation arising out of their sense of national uniqueness assuming the British liberal notions of indirect rule to preserve African traditional life while promoting gradualism in their Christianization and westernization. Their concerns for job protection promoted by the face of a larger and cheaper black proletariats. Under Apartheid different races where given rights. In practice the system was one of white supremacy, blacks having no representation in the central state parliament. Many of the provisions of Apartheid regarding labour, land segregation (reserves, homelands, Bantustans). Municipal segregation, social and educational separation. Apartheid built a virtually exclusive white franchise was put into place before the Nationalist victory of 1948, but after that date it was erected into a complete political, social and economic systems, beaches, lavatories, park benches etc. Its principal architect was Hendrik Verwoerd who was assassinated in 1966. The laws included the Probation of Mixed Marriages Act and the Population Registration Act of 1949; the Immorality Act and the Groups Act of 1950; the Prevention of Illegal Squatting Act of 1953; the Intention of these Acts where to separate white and black living areas, educational provision and social intercourse. Jobs were also reserved according to race. The Apartheid system was ultimately destroyed because of international pressure and that it failed to work by matching economic realities. Most of these laws were repealed after F.W De klerk became President in 1989. He announced the abandonment of the Afrikaner Apartheid programme and unbanned all black political parties.

➤ Agadir: A port on the Atlantic coast of Morocco which was visited in July 1911 by the German gunboat Panther, supposedly to protect German interest in Morocco threatened by the French, whom Kiderlen-Wacther had accused of acting contrary to the agreement reached in the 1906 Conference of Algeciras. It was alarmed by the presence of the Panther in a part relatively close to Gibraltar. They suspected the Germans of seeking to establish a naval presence in Agadir thereby posing a threat to British trade routes. This crisis came close to precipitating hostilities they where however averted.

➤ Algeciras Conference 1906: This conference was called to defuse the difference between France and Germany which derived from the first Moroccan Crisis. The Conference resulted in the acceptance by Germany, outmanoeuvred diplomatically by the French and particularly by the British, of the act of Algeciras. The Germans had hoped both to curb the growth of French Influences in Morocco and to harm the developing cordiality in relations between France and Britain. They however constrained under the Act to accent provisions whereby, with due respect to the authority of the Sultan of Morocco, France and Spain were authorised to police Morocco under the supervision of Swiss Inspector-General.

- The Algerian War of Independence (1954-62): It was mounted from a growing resentment against the French Colonial Rule in Algeria which was fuelled by Arab nationalism which gathered strength after the Second World War. It ignited the FLN (Front de liberation Nationale), expressed themselves on the night of the 1st of November 1954 when Algerian nationalist attacked French military and civilian targets, by 1956 guerrilla warfare became widespread on the rural areas by the late 1050's forming from over 100 000 nationalist guerrilla forces with Tunisian support. They were actively involved in the battle for Independence. The 400 000-500 000 strong French army under General Jacques Massu responded with harsh methods which led to wide-spread criticism and public opinion in France which began to turn. In May 1958 there was a revolt in the Algiers by the French Officers under General Massu who suspected that the Mendes France government would enter into negotiations with the FLN. This came close to triggering Civil War in France and which brought about the fall of the French Government. This then led to the inauguration of the fifth Republic of General de Gaulle on 1st June 1958 who promised self determination to Algeria later in there year despite subsequent attempts by right-wing French colonist, the army General Raoul Salon and the Organisation Arme'e Secrete (OAS) who tried to prevent the attainment of Algerian Independence, peace talks began at Evian-les-Bains in France in March 1962 with Ahmed Ben Bella as the first Premier of the new Algerian government.

- Apartheid (Afrikaans 'Apartness'): The policy of separate racial development in South Africa supported traditionally by the National Party and more recently the right-wing parties during the late 1980's. Their ideology has several roots on being the Boer concept of racial, cultural, and religious separation arising out of their sense of uniqueness; British liberal notions of Indirect Rule; the need to preserve African traditional life while promoting gradualism in their Christianisation and westernisation; and the concerns for job protection, promoted by White workers to maintain their status in the face of large and cheaper Black proletariat. Under the policy different races are given different rights. In practice, the system was one of white supremacy, Blacks having no representative in the Central State Parliament. Many of the provisions of Apartheid regarding labour, land segregation, social and educational separation and a virtually exclusive White Franchise, were in place before the Nationalist victory of 1948, but after that date it was erected into a complete political, social and economic system, down to the provision of petty apartheid relating to transport, beaches, Lavatories, park benches etc. Its principle architect Hendrik Verwoerd, was assassinated in 1966. At the end of the 80's F.W. De Klerk began the liberalization movement which resulted in the all political parties being unbanned and the election or Nelson Mandela in 1994 as President and the ANC winning the majority of the seats in the New South Africa parliament.

➢ Apartheid Laws: A body of legislation in the old South Africa which was passed by the National Party government after their victory of 1948. Apartheid was based on the combination of ideas derived from Boers sense of separateness and from the British Colonial practice of Indirect Rule. Earlier laws such as the Native Land Act of 1913 created a foundation for the extreme form of separation promoted by the nationalist. The laws included the prohibition of Mixed Marriages Act and the Populations Registration Act both in 1949; the immorality Act and the Group Area's Act of 1950; the prevention of illegal squatting Act 1951; the Bantu Authorities Act and Bantu Education Act of 1953. The intention of these Acts was to separate white and black living areas educational provision and social intercourse. Jobs were also reserved, according to race, but the apartheid system was ultimately destroyed because it failed to match economic realities. Most of these laws were repealed after F W De Klerk became President in 1989 and announced the abandonment of the Apartheid programme.

➢ Anglo-Egypt Treaty (1936): In 1922 the British government had issued a deal which recognized Egypt as an Independent sovereign state. Though the British retained the control of the Suez Canal, the right to keep troops in the Canal Zone and the condominium in the Sudan. The 1936 treaty gave more of the Subtance of Independence to Egypt. The British residents in Egypt lost their legal and financial privileges. The British occupation was formally ended and Egypt gained control of their armed forces for the first time since 1882. In wartime, the British had the right to reoccupy the country a right they exercised in 1939 just as the Second World War began.

- Arusha Declaration 29 January 1967: A document written under President Julius Nyerere's direction and accepted by Tanganyika African Union (TANU) National Executive Committee in Arusha. It set out the assumptions underlying Tanzania's version of African Socialism, emphasing the dignity and equality of people, the primary of rural production, self reliance, the importance of hard work and the role of the party. Later documents for education, self reliance, socialism and rural development came after the Arusha Declaration developed Nyerere's ideas of creating a uniquely African and Egalitarian Socialism in Africa, but it proved economically disastrous although for the most part, politically popular.

- AWB: Afikaanse Weestand Bewwering, Afrikaner Resistance Movement a Para-military group founded in 1973 and led by the late Eugene Terri Blanche who was murdered in 2009 by his own black worker over a dispute of pay and continuing racial abuse. The movement was prepared to support it aims of preserving white control over South Africa by force, they even attempted to storm-down the CODESSA meeting for all political parties set up by F.W De Klerk in the early 1990'sBarbary Coast: The coast of North Africa from Morocco to Tripolitania (Libya), famous for piracy between the Barbary States of Morocco, Algeria, Tunisia and Tripolitania take their name from Barbarossa, who led the Turkish conquest of the region in the 1530's, preventing Spanish invasion.

- Azania (Zanji): The names given by the ancient and medieval Greek and Arab geographers to the northern part of the East African Coast. 'Azania's' were the early Bantu speaking inhabitants of the Coast. In modern times, the name Azania has been used by some nationalist groups, especially the Pan-Africanist Congress, to denote a post-apartheid South Africa.

- Berber Hamito-Semitic speaking people of Egypt, Algeria, Libya, Tunisia and Morocco. They were originally settled in one area but the Bedouin Arabs who invaded North Africa in the 12th century turned many of them into nomads. Most Berber tribes ultimately accepted Islam, and in the 11th century formed themselves into a military federation known as The Almoravids, who conquered the medieval state of Ghana, Morocco, Algeria and South Spain. In the 12th century their power began wane, and the Almohads, a new group influenced by Sufism by 1169 came to command the entire Maghib to Tripoli, as well as Muslim Spain. The Almonhads

Empire declined in the 13<sup>th</sup> century. Today many of them work as migrants in Southern Europe the best known groups include the Kabyle, Shluh and Taureg.

> Biafran War 1967-70: Biafra is a South- Eastern province of Nigeria which is inhabited by the Igabo people. They attempted to break away from the federation of Nigeria under the Leadership of Colonel Ojukwas, which precipitated the civil war which was called the Biafran War of 1967-70 which saw two military coups in 1966 which left Nigeria racked by ethnic division. In May 1967 Lt-Col Chukuvemoka Ojukwa was mandated by the Ibo consultative assembly to declare the Eastern Region of Nigeria Independent as the state of Biafra Civil War then broke out as the Federal government led by Gowon sought to keep Nigeria one. It was not until Jan 1970 that the Federal forces prevailed and with Ojukwa exiled peace was restored in Nigeria.

> Black Consciousness Movement (South Africa): A loose movement formed by Steve Biko in 1969, when he led African students out of the multiracial Nation Union of South African Students and founded the South African Student Organisation from this emerged the Black Peoples Convention in 1972 which sought to create cooperation in social and cultural fields among all non-white peoples. Banned in 1976, most of its leaders were imprisoned in 1977 and Biko died in police custody soon afterwards.

> Black Saturday (26<sup>th</sup> January 1952): After guerrilla attacks on their buses in Egypt, the British acted against suspects, including the Egyptian police. British forces surrounded police headquarters at Ismailia and called on the police to surrender, they refused and 50 were killed in the attack on their headquarters. The next day Black Saturday Egyptian people led by the Muslim Brotherhood burnt down British and Foreign shops and restaurants in the centre of Cairo. Egyptian troops did not intervene to bring the situation under control until evening. King Farouk I and the government blamed each other for the delay, which brought about a period of instability. This led free Officers to bring forward the coup they had planned to occur in 1954 to July 1952, forcing King Farouk into exile. The Free Officers of Egypt were a small group of army officers formed after the fiasco of the 1948 war, who were bent on the expulsion of the British from Egypt and the removal of the politician in power at the time. In the aftermath of the riots of the Black Saturday January 1952, The Free Officers were firstly led by

Neguib, Mohammed and then Gamal Abd al Nasser who took control of the country. Nasser went on to run the country until his death in 1969. The Free Officers played a leading role in Egypt throughout the period until the June War of 1967 when, with the growing rift between Abd al Hakim Amer and Nasser which led to Amers subsequent suicide, the solidarity of the Free Officers was broken.

➤ The Boers Wars: Blood River, the battle of Blood River in December 1838 it was a battle in which the Boers of the then Trekker republic of Natalia defeated the Zulu. Andries Pretorius with a commando of 500 men avenged the killing of Piet Retief and attacks on Boer settlements ordered by Dingane the ZULU King. In February of 1838. The battle has remained a central aspect of Boer mythology in relation to Afrikaner ever since and has become the subject of annual Commorations. The Boer wars of 1880-1881 and 1899-1902 these two wars were fought against the British for the mastery of Southern Africa. The British had made several attempts to re-incorporate the Boers, who had left the Cape Colony in the Great Trek within the South African Confederation. The first Boer War ended with the defeat of the British at Majuba Hill, and the signing of the Pretoria and London Convention of 1881 and 1884. In 1896 the Jamison Raid was a dumsy private effort to achieve the same objective. The second Boer War can be divided into three phases: (1) October 1899-January 1900 saw a series of Boer successes, including the sieges of Ladysmith, Kimberly and Mafeking, as well as victories at Stormberg, Modder River, Magerstontein, Colenso and Moderspruit. (2) February-August 1900 were counter-offensives from the British led by Lord Roberts which included the raising of the sieges, the victory at Paardeberg and the capture of Pretoria (3) September 1900- May 1902 saw a period of guerrilla warfare mounted by the Boer commando who raided Isolated British units and lines of communication. The Boers effectively won the peace at the Vereeniging Peace of 1902 the peace treaty which ended the Boer War was signed at Pretoria. The Boers won three important concessions (1) An amnesty for those who had raised in revolt within the Cape Colony (2) A promise that the British would deny the franchise to Africans until after the Boer Republics were returned to representative government in and (3) An additional financial support for reconstruction. They also maintained the control of native affairs; won back representative government I 1907, and then formed the Federation of South Africa on their own terms in 1910. On the other hand British interest in

South Africa were protected and despite internal strains. The Union of South Africa entered both World Wars on the British side. The peace ensured that there would be no significant change in the political relationship of whites and blacks in South Africa forming the foundation for the creation of Apartheid.

➢ The British South African Company: A company formed by Cecil John Rhodes which at the time used a series of concessions from King Lobengula and other Central African Chiefs in order for Rhodes to secure a Royal Charter from the British government in 1889. It invaded Mashonaland in 1890 and by 1900 the company ruled much of Central Africa despite considerable African resistance. In 1923-4 its territories were divided into Northern Rhodesia (Zambia after 1964) and Southern Rhodesia (Zimbabwe after 1980). It managed to retain the rights to extensive mineral rights in both countries to date.

➢ Broederbond: A secret Afrikaner organisation founded in 1918. Membership was limited to male Afrikaners and was by invitation only and was intended to integrate potential Afrikaner political ambitions and then to protect them. Since the early 1980's it became some what more open as it split between its reformist (Verligte) and its reactionary (Verkrampte) wings.

➢ Buganda: one of the states of Uganda, occupying territory on the north-west shore of Lake Victoria. It began to expand in the 17th century, and was very powerful by the 19th century. It was involved in the trade in ivory, slaves and other commodities with the Nyamwezi in the 18th century, and later became a focus of the struggle among Muslim, Catholic and Protestant parties. The British ruled Uganda through the indirect rule system, and the continuing existence of the Kingdom caused serious strains for independent Uganda.

➢ Burundi Civil War: The Burundi Civil War was armed was an armed conflict lasting from 1993 to 2005. The civil war was the result of long standing ethnic division between the Hutu and the Tutsi tribes of Burundi. The conflict began following the first multiparty elections in the country since Independence from the Belgium's in 1962 and is seen a formally ending with the swearing in of Pierre Nkurunzia in August 2005. The estimated death toll stands at 3 000 000 killed.

- ➤ Cairo conference Egypt (1921): Convened by Winston Churchill this conference had as its objective the consideration of the many problems afflicting the middle East, particularly those thrown up by World War I. Discussions covered such questions as defence in the area and the treatment of the Iraqi Kurds on which no decision was reached, but the most important result of the conference was the emergence of the two Hashimite rulers: The King of Iraq and the Amir of Transjordan later became the King of Jordan after the creation of the state of Israel and the addition to the former Transjordan of the West Bank and the Old City of Jerusalem.

- ➤ Cairo Conference Egypt (1943): A meeting held between Winston Churchill and Roosevelt which was attended by Chiang Kai-Shek Chaing was anxious that the allies continue to support the war efforts in China at a time when they were considering inviting Stalin to bring the USSR into the Pacific War and whether to concentrate on capturing the Pacific Island from where Japan might be bombed rather than from Chinese airfields. Both developments would render the China Theatre marginal. Chiang was handicapped by both Anglo-American differences over strategy and by Roosevelt's increasing hostility to Chiang's regime, which was seen as hopelessly corrupt. The Cairo Conference was a significant turning-point in Washington's policy towards Chiang Kai-Shek; hitherto consider a crucial actor in the war against Japan. Chiang did not receive the assurances he desired, while later in the same year Stalin pledged to enter the war in return for privileges in the Manchuria (China).

- ➤ Camp David Accords (1978): Documents signed by Answar Sadt, then the President of Egypt, and Menachem Begin, then the Prime Minister of Israel as preliminary to signing of the peace treaty (1979) between the two countries. It was witnessed by President Jimmy Carter at Camp David, Maryland USA, in September 1978. Regarded by many as a triumph of the US diplomacy. Egypt was given back the Sinai Desert which had been captured by the Israeli in the 1976 One day War.

- ➤ Cape Coloured or Coloured: A term used by the South African government to refer to a group of mixed descent, arising from the unions of Europeans with slaves from Madagascar, Mozambique, or the East or Khoikoi (Hottentots). They number about 2.5 million people 9% of the total population (Check correct current population figures). They mainly lived in the towns and rural areas of the

Western Cape Province. They were culturally akin to white South Africa, most Coloured speak Afrikaans and are Christian, with a small Muslim minority (Cape Malays). In South Africa's racial hierarchy, they were ranked between Europeans and Black Africans. They lived in separate areas on the outskirts, with their own schools and other facilities. They had limited rights within the old Apartheid system. They are mostly farm labourers, factory workers, and artisan with a small middle class. Coloureds rejected the classification Cape Coloured and refer to themselves as the 'So called Cape Coloureds'.

➢ Carthage: An Ancient town in Tunisia, North Africa, now a Suburb of Tunis; a world heritage site. Reputedly founded by the Phoenicians in 814 B.C, it was destroyed by Rome following the Punic Wars (146 B.C) but was refounded by Ceaser and Octavian (29 B.C). Carthage was restored as a capital by the? Vanchals? (A.D 439-533), but was again destroyed by the Arabs in 699 A.D.

➢ Central African Federation (1953-63): A federal territory established by the British government to bring together the administration of Northern and Southern Rhodesia and Nyasaland (now Zambia, Zimbabwe and Malawi). The federation was designed to act as a counterweight to South Africa, which had been dominated by the Afrikaner Nationalist since after their elections of 1948. It was established to encourage investment into the region, theoretically its societies its societies and governments were developed on the basis of racial partnership. In reality it became a means for the extension of white settler's power by stimulating togetherness. In turn stimulated African Nationalist resistance and an emergency were declared after disturbances broke out in Nyasaland in 1959, together with strikes and political activism in Northern Rhodesia. After the Devlin and Monckton commission reports that the Federation of Zambia; Malawi and the Unilateral Declaration of Independence (UDI) in Rhodesia by Ian Smith broke up.

➢ Central African Republic Bush War: The Central African Republic bush war began with the rebellion by the Union of Democratic Forces for Unity (UFDR) which is led by Michel Detodia, after the current President of the Central African Republic Fracois Bozize seized power in 2003; the real fighting began in 2004. The civil war may be connected to the Darfur Conflict in neighbouring Sudan. So far around 10 000 people have been displaced. The UFDR consist of three allies The Groud d`action, Partriotique Pour la Liberation de Centrafrique (GAPLC) the Movement des Liberateurs Centrafricains pourla Justice (MLCJ), and the Front de`mocratique Centrafrican (FDC). This alliance signed a peace agreement in April 2007. According to the Human Rights Watch (HRW) hundreds of civilians have been killed, more than 10 000 houses burnt and approximately 212 000 people have fled their homes to live in desperate conditions deep in the bush in Northern Central African Republic. Further negotiations resulted in an agreement in 2008 for reconciliation, a unity government and local elections in 2009 and they held elections in 2010. It is currently being led by

➢ Chad Civil War 2005-present: The current civil war in Chad began in December 2005, the conflict involves the Chadian government forces and several Chadian rebels groups these include the United Front for Democratic Change (UFDC); United Forces for Development and Democracy (UFDD); Gathering of Forces for Change (GFC) and the National Accord of Chad (NAC). The conflict has also involved the Janjaweed, while Sudan allegedly supported the rebels while Libya mediated in the conflict. The government of Chad estimated in January 2006 that 614 Chadians citizens were killed in cross-border raids. On 8th February 2006 the Tripoli Agreement was signed which stopped the fighting for approximately two months. However fighting persisted after that, leading to several new agreement attempts. In 2007 a rift between the main Zaghawa and Tama tribes of Chad emerged the Zaghawa tribe, to which Chad's President Idriss Deby belongs accused the Sudanese government of supporting members of the rival Tama tribe. The Civil War has deep connection to the war in the Darfur and the Central African Republic Bush War.

➢ Chama Cha Mapinduzi (CCM): At times referred to as the Revolutionary Part of Tanzania, this party was formed in 1977 by the merger of the Tanganyika African National Union (TANU) and the Afro-Shirazi Party; it became the only legal political party in Tanzania. It became relatively pluralist with its activities with women, the youth and they set up local branches at grass roots.

➢ Committee of National Liberation (Algeria): The committee set up by Charles de Gaulle on the 3rd of June 1943, through which the Algerians were promised a full voice in the country. The failure to fulfil this promise was, more than any other single factor, responsible for the hardening of native Algerian resistance to the presumptions of the French in Algeria, which eventually resulted in the Algerian War of Independence.

➤ Conservative Party of South Africa: A South African party formed in 1982 by reactionary (Verkrampte) members of the National Party who had been expelled from the Parliament. It was led by Andries Treurtnicht and after the 1987 general election, became the chief opposition party in the white parliament and opposed the liberalization measures undertaken by President De Klerk.

➤ De Beers Consolidated Mines: Is the diamond mining company formed by Cecil Rhodes in 1887 from the amalgamation of several companies operating at Kimberly, (Cape Province). The De Beers mine was one of the original diamond concessions named after the Boer Farmer on whose land the diamond were found. Rhodes and his associate Rudd formed the De Beers Mining Company in 1880 and set about the gradual acquisition of other mines. Kimberly became virtually a company town and by 1900 De Beers was contributing 50% of all the export of the Cape Colony. Rhodes used both his personal wealth derived from the company to purse his dreams in the Rand and to form the British South African Company to pursue his other dreams in Central Africa. De Beers developed the closed compound system for migrant black labourers which became a major feature of South African urban life. De Beers became one of the most powerful companies in the 20th century in the South Africa and the World Diamond market.

➤ Economic Community of West African States (ECOWAS): An organisation formed in May 1975 by 15 Western African states through the Treaty of Lagos it was made up by Benin; The Gambia; Ghana; Guinea-Bissau; Ivory Coast (Cote d'Ivoire), Liberia; Mali; Mauritania; Niger; Nigeria; Senegal; Sierra Leone; Togo; and Burkina Faso. Cape Verde joined in 1977. Its headquarters is based in Abuja, Nigeria. Its principle objective are the ending of restrictions on trade between them and the establishment of a common customs tariff, the harmonization of economic and industrial policies and equalisation of the development of member states. In 1990 it set up a standing Mediation Committee to mediate disputes between member states. It has also supported the free movement of people and also overseen a collaboration military involvement in Liberia.

> Egypt: A Republic in North-East Africa, the history of Egypt can be traced as far back as c.6000 B.C, to the Neolithic cultures on the River Nile. A unified Kingdom embracing Lower and Upper Egypt which was created in 3100 B.C ruled by a Pharaoh Dynasties; the pyramids at El Giza were constructed during the fourth the Dynasty. Egyptian power was greatest during the New Empire period (1567-1085 B.C.). It became a Persian province during the 6th century Before Christ and was conquered by Alexander the Great in the 4th century Before Christ. Ptolemaic Pharaohs ruled Egypt until 30 B.C. It was conquered by Arabs in A.D 672. It was occupied by France under Napoleon from 1798 until 1801. The Suez Canal was constructed in 1869. A revolt 1879 was, put down by the British in 1882. Egypt became a British protectorate in 1914 and declared its independence in 1922. It was used as a base for Allied forces during World War II. King Farouk was deposed by Nasser in 1952, and Egypt was declared a Republic the following year. An attack on Israel, which was counter followed by an attack by Israel forces in 1976, resulted in the loss of the Sinai Peninsula and control of part of the Suez Canal. It was regained following negotiations in the 1970's. In 1981, President Sadat was assassinated and relations between Arab nations became strained, but improved throughout the 1980's. In the early 1990's there were violent attacks and clashes between Muslim and Coptic Christians. Egypt has recently had a people popular uprising against Mubarak who had been in power for over 30 years. People filled Tharir square from 25 January 2011 the Egyptian Revolution in which the participants placed emphasis on the peaceful nature of the struggle, mainly comprised a campaign of civil resistance, which featured a series of demonstrations, marches, acts of civil disobedience and labour strikes. Millions of prostestors from a variety of socio-economic and religious backgrounds demanded the resignation Hosni Mubarak. Despite being predominantly peaceful in nature the revolution was not without violent clashes between security forces and protestors. The campaign took place in Cairo; Alexandria and other cities in Egypt. The people occupied Tharir square until the 11th of February 2011 following weeks of determined popular protest and pressure Mubarak resigned from Office.

➤ Ethiopia: Formerly Abyssinia it is country in the North-East Africa. It is the oldest independent country in Sub-Saharan Africa, and the first African country to be Christianised. Abyssinian Independence was recognised by the League of Nations in 1923, but after the invasion by Italy in 1935 to 1941, when Emperor Haile Selassie returned from exile. A military coup led to led to the establishment of the Provisional Military Administrative Council (PMAC) in 1974, and the left-wing opposition was met by mass arrests and executions in 1977-8. In addition to conflict with Somalia over the Ogaden District during the 1970's and 1980's there was internal division with separatist Eritreans and Tigerean Forces, who secured victories over government troops in the early 1980's while the country suffered severe famine. PMAC dissolved in 1987, with the transfer of power to the Peoples Democratic Republic, but an attempted coup in 1989 and renewed famine in 1992. Eritrea secured independence in 1993.

➤ Eritrea Liberation Front (ELF): A movement seeking independence from Ethiopia founded in 1958. Eritrea an Italian Colony from 1884 was Federated with Ethiopia at the request of the UN in 1952 and then incorporated as a province in 1962. This galvanised the Front into action and despite some divisions, it managed, through support from the Eastern Bloc and some Arab countries, to prevent its destruction both while Haile Selassie was Emperor and when Mengistu became President. The collapse of the Dergue in 1991 advanced its position.

➤ Fanti States: Separate traditional states, each under the authority of a royal chief in Southern Ghana. The Fanti are Kwa-speaking framers and fishermen, but formerly they traded with the Europeans in coastal towns such as Elmina and the Cape Coast.

➤ Fashoda Incident (1898): The settlement of Fashoda (now Kodok) on the Upper White Nile was the scene of a major Anglo-French crisis in the year. French forces under Captain Jean Baptiste Marchand had reached the Nile after an 18 month journey from Brazzaville. The British, who were in the process of retaking Sudan, issued an ultimatum; France was not prepared to go to war, and Marchand was ordered to withdraw. The incident destroyed French ambitions for a trans-continental African Empire and confirmed British mastery of the Nile region.

➢ Front de Liberation Nationale (FLN): An organisation founded in the early 1950's, which campaigned and fought for Algerian Independence from France, under the leadership of Mohammed Ben Bella. The war with FLN led to the collapse of the French fourth Republic in 1958, and the return to power of de Gaulle. Frances inability to defeat FLN led to the Evian Conference in 1962, and aided the completion of the Algerian Independence.

➢ Frente Nacional de Liberatiqao de Angola (FNLA): Formed in 1962 it established a government in exile under Holden Roberto in Zaire and with US assistance was active in Northern Angola, especially after the Portuguese left the country. Its poor leadership and reduced US support weakened it effectiveness and it ceased operation in the early 1980's.

➢ Freedom Charter: The policy document adopted by the Congress Alliance (June 1955), when 3000 opposition delegates from all regions of South Africa met to co-ordinate policies and which was issued by the ANC in 1956. It set out a non racial policy for South Africa, emphasizing its Fabians principle as well as its commitment to racial equality.

➢ Free Officers of Egypt: A small group of army officers formed after the fiasco of the 1948 war, which was bent on the expulsion of the British from Egypt and the removal of the politicians in power at the time. In the aftermath of the riots of Black Saturday (Jan 1952), the Free Officers, fearing that King Farouk might be about to have them arrested, rose and forced Farouk in to Abdication in July 1952. The Free Officers were first led by Neguib Mohammed and then Gamal Abd al-Nasser who took control of the country. Nasser went on to run the country until his death in 1969. The Free Officers played a leading role in Egypt throughout the period until the June War of 1967 when with the growing rift between Abd-al Hakim Amer and Nassser. The subsequent suicide of Amer and further internal fighting led to the solidarity of the Free-Officer been broken.

➢ Free Officers Movement (Libya): Libya became independent in 1951 with a Sanusi Leader Amir Idris as King. His regime was however soon condemned by students and young army officers as corrupt for being dependent on foreign support. Inspired by the Pan-Arab and socialist doctrines of Gamal Abd al-Nasser of Egypt and their Ba'ath Party. The Free Officers Movement, consisting of middle-ranking officers and NCOs' whom where led by Muammar al-Gaddafi, their seized power and set up a Revolutionary Command Council that established a military dictatorship which exist to-date. Foreign banks and business were nationalised and business were nationalised and all other political parties and trade unions were all outlawed.

➢ Frente de Liberation de Mozambique, Mozambique Liberation front (FRELIMO): Founded in 1962, it was led by Edurado Mondlane who was assassinated in Tanzania. The leadership passed on to Samora Machel. FERLIMO waged a successful guerrilla war against the Portuguese. They established liberated zones in which they formed rudimentary governmental structure were established. At independence in 1975, it became the only legal party in Mozambique.

➢ German East Africa Company: The Company established by Germans to exploit it's newly acquired territory of Tanganyika. It acquired a Charter on the British Model in 1885 which saw Karl Peters and his associates collect treaties from East African Chiefs. However the Charter was lost in 1892 because Peters Company proved unable to cope with the Swahili and African resistance to the German East African Company rule.

➢ German South-West Africa Company: A company formed to exploit the German Colony in South-West Africa (Namibia) proclaimed by Bismarck in 1884 outlining the trading positions of Adolf Luderitz. The company was never chartered and was always under-capitalised. In the 1890's it faced competition from more financially secure British company the South West Africa Company.

➢ Great Trek: the movement of parties of Boers (Voortrekkers) which made them the masters of the large tracts of the interior of Southern Africa. Objecting to British suzerainty, they began to leave the Cape Colony in 1836 in separate trekking groups. Two parties were wiped out by black African resistance and malaria when they headed for the Delagoa Bay in Mozambique. Some settled in the Transvaal, where they were threatened by the Ndebele. One party in Natal was massacred by the Zulu, an event avenged by the battle of Blood River in 1938. When the British annexed Natal in 1843, the majority of the Boers returned to the interior. The British made several unsuccessful attempts to resolve the division in the area, but when the region was reunited it was largely under Boer control.

> Guinea-Bissau Civil War: It was triggered by an attempted coup d'état against President Joa`o Bernardo Vieira led by Brigadier-General Ansumane Mane` in June 1998. Clashes between government forces backed by neighbouring states forces and the rebels.

> Herero Revolt (1907): A resistance movement by Bantu-speaking people in Namibia, crushed by the Germans with great brutality. They participated in the struggle for Namibian independent against South African rule.

> Humanism: The philosophy espoused by Kenneth Kaunda of Zambia. It was based upon Julius Nyerere's philosophy of 'Ujama' it aimed to find a specifically African conception of an African's place in society and the economy in which human dignity and equality were the central principles. It was never taken as seriously as Nyerere's writings as a blueprint for public policy.

> Igbo or Ibo: A people of Eastern Nigeria, living in many small and traditionally autonomous communities within a common culture present day population of millions, they dominated agricultural trade in Nigeria, and produced the earliest bronze art in the region. They also established the short lived state of the Biafra 1960-70, during which time the genocide of the Igbo Ibo living in other parts of Nigeria occurred.

> Ilorin: A state lying to the north of Yoruba-Land in Central Nigeria which resisted Europeans missionary and trading encroachment in the 19th century, but was conquered by the Royal Niger Company and acted as a further springboard for the conquest of the Northern Emirates Muslim Ilorin which was an outlier of the Sokoto caliphate. It was annexed to British rule in 1896 when Sir George Goldie undertook a campaign against it its neighbour Nupe.

> Imperial British East Africa Company: A British Company founded and chartered to rule a large area of East Africa in 1888. It was designed to ward off the German and French threats to the area and maintain British access to Lake Victoria Uganda and the Upper Nile. However it was seriously undercapitalised and could not find the resources to develop the region, creating an infrastructure, or

withstand African resistance. It was wound up in 1894 and its territories became the protectorates of Britain (Crown Colonies) of Kenya and Uganda.

➤ Inkatha Freedom Party: A loose political organisation based in Zululand (South Africa) and answerable to Chief Gatsha Buthelezi which in the 1970's and 80's offered an opposition to apartheid but then became the vehicle for Zulu nationalism and sometimes violent antagonist to the ANC. It received clandestine support from the police and the government of F.W De Klerk.

➤ Isandlhwanga Battle (1878): A notorious reverse for the British in the Zulu War of 1879, through mismanagement an entire British regiment was virtually destroyed by the Zulu using their traditional tactics due to the facts their failed to open their ammunition boxes. It was allayed only by the victory of Ulindi later in the same year. (Check Zulu Wars).

➤ Ivorian Civil War: The civil war that began on September 19th 2002, although most of the fighting ended by the late 2004. The country remains remains split in to two with the rebel held North and the government held South. French troops were supposed to be brought into Cote d`Ivore to help resolve the situation. But they played a key role in worsening this tension by destroying the 2 aircrafts of the Ivorian Army the crafts their used for bombing the rebels camps. Hostilities increased and raids on foreign troops and many said that the United Nations and the French military had failed to calm the civil war; however the Ivorian national football team was credited with helping to secure a temporary truce, when it qualified for the World Cup. The United Nations Operations in Co`te d`Ivore began after the Civil War calmed down but the peace keepers have faced complicated situation and were outnumbered by the civilians and rebels. A peace agreement to end the conflict was signed on October 2010 after being delayed 6 times, fighting resumed on 24th February 20011 over the impasse on the elections results with the new force rebels capturing Zouan-Hounien and clashes in Abodo, Yamoussoukro and around Anyama.

➤ Jameson Raid ( Dec 1875- Jan 1896): An expedition against the South African Republic, which was supposed to link up with a revolt by white workers on the rand and attempt to topple the government of President Kruger. Leander Starr Jameson who was an administrator for the South Africa Company at Fort Salisbury led the detachment of British South African police into Transvaal, but they were easily defeated and arrested. The German Emperor, William II sent a telegraph of congratulations to Paul Kruger. This incident caused a major government crisis in Britain as well as its contributions to the tensions that led to the Boer Wars.

➤ June 16th Soweto Students Uprising: It was a student disturbance which took place in the Transvaal African Township of SOWETO (Southern Western Townships). When several hundreds of students were killed resisting the teaching of all subjects in Afrikaans in schools. The township remained a source of tension and violence in South Africa leading up to the freedom of Nelson Mandela in 1989-90. It then turned into internal tribal-infighting and blood-shed leading up to the elections of 1994 between the Zulu migrant favouring Bhutulezi Inkata party versus the majority ANC local supporters.

➤ Kabra Bassa: A major dam and hydroelectric plant in Mozambique, Kabra Bassa was a set of cataracts on the Zambezi just above the town of Tete which were seen by David Livingstone on his second African Journey between 1858 and 1863. In the late 1960's the Portuguese rulers of Mozambique embarked upon the building of a dam, funded by foreign investment, which would supply electricity to South Africa and to create a vast Lake which would provide irrigation for new areas of white settlement in the Zambezi Valley. FRELIMO saw it a symbol of continuing white domination and from 1968 began a campaign to sabotage it. They failed, but pinned down Portuguese troops in its defence, South African military and Air Force were also involved.

➤ Kabyle: A Berber people of Algeria Organised into different castes with Serfs, they speak Kablye a Hamito-Semitic Language and are predominantly Muslim. They live in villages, growing grains and olives and herd goats they amount to about 2 million people.

➤ KaNgwane: A national state or non-independent Black homeland in Natal Province, South Africa. It gained self-governing status in 1971. It ceased to exist in May 1994 after the first all race election in South Africa.

➤ Kenya African National Union (KANU): The political party that led Kenya into independence in 1963. It was founded in 1960 as successor to the Kikuyu Central Association of 1929 and the Kenya African Union of 1947. The Kenya African Democratic Union (KADU) was a rival body which represented mainly the non-Kikuyu groups KANU won the first Kenyan elections with Kenyatta Jomo Kamau Ngengi becoming Kenya's First President. He attempted to bring KADU into Coalition but failed.

➢ Kenyan Crisis 2007-2008: This crisis was caused by the economic and humanitarian crisis that erupted in Kenya after incumbent President Mwai Kikabi was declared the winner of the presidential elections held in December 27th 2007, supporters of Kikabi's opponent Raila Odinga of the Orange Democratic Movement, alleged electoral manipulation. This was widely confirmed by international observers, perpetrated by both parties in the elections. In part all this due to ethnic and geographical diversity of the ODM coalition, no one narrative can explain the reaction of opposition supporters to the announcement of Kabaki's swearing in. In addition to staging several nonviolent protests, opposition supporters went on a violent rampage in several parts of the country, most noticeably in the Odinga's homeland of Nyanza Province and the slums of Nairobi, part of his Langata constituency. Police shot a number of demonstrators, including a few in front of TV news cameras causing more violence directed towards the police. Targeted ethnic violence escalated and at first directed mainly against the Kikuyu people the community of which Kibaki is a member. The violence peaked with the killing of over 30 unarmed civilians in a church near Eldoret on new year's day. Tension in the Rift Valley have caused violence in several previous Kenyan elections mostly notably in the 1992 Kenyan elections. Some of the Kikuyu people engaged in violence against tribal groups supportive of Odinga, primarily the Luos and Katenjin especially in the areas surrounding Nakura and Naivasha. In Mombasa, Muslim Kenyans took to the street to protest the electoral manipulation and air their own grievances, though ethnic tensions played much less of a role in these protests, looters also struck a number of states in Mombasa, the slums of Nairobi saw some of the worst violence, most of it ethnically motivated attacks, some simple outrage at extreme poverty and some actions of criminal gangs, the violence continued sporadically for several months, particularly in the Rift Valley. Former United Nations Secretary General Kofi Annan arrived in the country nearly a month after the elections and successfully brought the two sides to the negotiating table. On February 28th 2008, Kibaki and Odinga signed a power-sharing agreement called the National Accord and Reconciliation ACT which establishes the office of Prime Minister and creates a coalition government. The power-sharing cabinet, headed by Odinga as Prime Minster was eventually named on April 13th 2008 after lengthy negotiations over its composition it was sworn in on 17th April 2008.

➢ Katanga: The Southernmost Province of Zaire, which is rich in minerals. In 1960 when the Congo (Zaire) achieved independence from Belgium. Katanga (Shaba) attempted to secede under the leadership of Moise Tshombe. In the ensuing chaos the government of Patrice Lumumba was overthrown. Lumumba was assisnated in 1961, and the unitary state was later re-created under the military leadership of President Mobuto.

➢ Khosian People: They inhabited the Cape of Good Hope where they encountered the Dutch when they landed at the Cape to trade and after their settlement of 1652. They are made up of the Khoi-Khoi or Hottentots and San or Bushman people. The Khoi-Khoi were pastoralist, while the San were hunters-gathers. However, there was a great deal of marital and economic interaction between them and they are generally grouped together, they speak a language with a distinctive click sound which survives among the Bushmen and has had their clicks being used by the Bantu language of the Nguni people. The Dutch-Boer traded amicably with the Khosian but relations soon became bitter and violent. The Khoi, whose decentralised political system made it difficult for them to combine for military success thus were devastated by the War, their loss of their cattle through the drought and raids. There was also an outbreak of smallpox among them. The Khoi are now one element in the Cape-Coloured Community while the San are marginalised in the Kalahari Desert. In the 18th Century Europe the word 'Hottentot' was used to mean any uncivilized person or people.

➢ Kikuyu Central Association (KCA): A society founded in Kenya in 1922 under the leadership of Harry Thuku Jomo Kenyatha the nationalist Leader. He became the President of Kenya but began as the Secretary-General of the KCA, which became the basis of African politics in the British Colony. It took up African grievances such as the European occupation of the Kikuyu Lands in the 'White Lands' and the missionary campaign to abolish female circumcision. It established the Kikuyu Leadership of Nationalism in Kenya but was banned during the World War II. The Kenya African Union emerged as its successor in 1944.

➢ Kilwa: A great trading town on the coast of Southern Tanzania, which acted as the major entry point of the trade of the interior of East-Central Africa with the middle East and the Indian Ocean. Kilwa owed its rise to the migration of the Shirazi merchants from the Persian Gulf in the 12th Century. By the early 14th Century it had supplanted Mogadishu as the greatest port on the coast, the southern limit of the Arab traders who used the annual monsoons to connect Africa to Asia. It flourished for the succeeding two centuries until it was sacked by the Portuguese, it remaining ruins are a testimony to its magnificence in its heydays with palaces, mosques and warehouses built of coral. It became a slaving port in the 18th Century.

➢ Kimberly Siege: The 1899-1900 sieges by the Boer forces who attempted to pen up the British and secure control of vital lines of communication, the siege lasted from the middle of October 1899 until February 1900, when the town was relieved by General French troops.

➢ Kivu Conflict: The Kivu conflict is an armed conflict between the military of the Democratic Republic of Congo (FARDC) and the Hutu power group the Democratic Forces for the Liberation of Rwanda (FDLR); The United Nations mission to the Democratic Republic of Congo also became involved in the conflict. Until March 2009 the main combatant group against the FARDC was the rebel Tutsi Forces formally under the command of Laurent Nkunda (National Congress for the Defence of the People (CNDP). CNDP is sympathict to the Banyamutenge in Eastern Congo, an ethnic Tutsi group and to the Tutsi-dominated government of Rwanda. It was opposed by the FDLR, by the DRC's army and by the United Nations forces. Laurent Nkunda was an officer in the rebel Rally for Congolese Democracy (RCD), Goma faction in the Second Congo War (1998-2002). In 2003, with the official end to the war. Nkunda joined the new integrated national army of the transitional government as Colonel and was promoted to General in 2004. He soon rejected the authority of the government and retreated with some of the RCD-GOMA troops to the Masisi forest in Nord Kivu. Minerals such as cassiterite, gold and Colton which is used for electronic equipment and cell phones are an important export for the Congo. The organisation Global Witness says "western companies sourcing minerals are buying them from traders who finance rebel and government troop. A UN resolution states that anyone supporting illegal Congolese armed groups through illicit trade of natural resources should be subjected to sanctions including travel restrictions and an asset freeze. Later in 2004, Nkunda's Forces began clashing with the DRC army in Sud-Kivu and by May 2004, occupied Bakavu where he was accused of committing war crimes. In 2005 Nkunda called for the overthrowing of the government due to corruption and increasing numbers of RCD-Goma soldiers deserted the DRC army to join his forces. In 2006 January, his troops clashed with DRC army forces, also accused of war crimes by the MONUC. In late June 2006, Nkunda became subject to United Nations Security Council restrictions. During both the first and second rounds of the contested and violent 2006 general elections. Nkunda had said that he would respect the results. In November 25th 2006, however nearly a day before the Supreme Court ruled that Joseph Kabila had won the presidential elections second round, Nkunda's forces undertook a sizable offensive in Sake against the DRC army 11th Brigade also clashing with MONUC peacekeepers. The UN has since called on the DRC government to negotiate with Nkunda and the Interior Minister General Denis Kalume was sent to eastern DRC to begin negotiations. In December 7th 2006 RCD-Goma troops attacked DRC army positions in Nord Kivu with military assistance from the MONUC. Approximately 12 000 Congolese civilians fled the DRC to the Kisoro District in Uganda. In 2007 Nkunda's men raided 10 secondary schools and four primary schools where they took the children by force in order to make them join their ranks. According to the United Nations officials girls are taken as sex slaves, boys are used as fighters in violation of International law. In 2007 October the government set a deadline for Nkunda's troops to begin to disarm. This deadline passed without action, on 17th October, President Joseph Kabila ordered the military to prepare to disarm Nkunda forces forcibly. When government forces allied with Mai Mai around Bun advanced on Nkunda stronghold of Kichanga, thousands of civilians fled the fighting. In early November 2007 Nkunda forces captured the town of Nyanzele, about 100km north of Goma. The statement made by the United Nations Mission in the Democratic Republic of Congo was that it was willing to offer artillery support to the government forces. In a regional conference held in Addis Ababa the United States of America; Burundi; Rwanda; and Uganda pledged to support the Congolese government and not support negative forces widely seen as a code for Nkunda Forces. Nkunda sated in December 14th that he was open to peace talks. The government called such talks on 20th December to be held from December 27th 2007 to January 5th 2008. These peace talks were then postponed to be held from January 6th to January 14th 2008. Nkunda's group did attend but walked out in January 2008 after an alleged attempted arrest of one of their members. They later returned to the talks. The talks schedule was extended to until 21st January 2008 and then to 22nd January 2008 an agreement appeared to be within reach, it was further extended to 23rd January 2008 over final disagreement regarding war crimes cases. The peace deal was signed on 23rd January 2008 and included provisions for an immediate ceasefire, the phased withdrawal of all rebels' forces in North Kivu province, the resettlement of thousands of villagers and immunity for Nkunda's forces. In October 26th 2008 Nkunda's rebels seized a majority camp along with Virunga National Park for use as a base to launch attacks from. This occurred after the peace treaty failed with the resultant fighting displacing thousands of people. On October 27th riots began around the United Nations compound in Goma and civilians pelted the building with rocks and Molotov Cocktails claiming the UN had done nothing to prevent the Rebel advance. On October 29th the rebels declared a unilateral ceasefire as they approached Goma. Despite the ceasefire the situation remained volatile; according to World Vision workers had to flee to the Rwandan boarder in order to work. On October 30th and violence by Congolese Soldiers, some of them drunk continued in Goma, Nkunda called again for direct talks with the Congolese government, also stating that he would create a 'humanitarian aid corridor', a non fire zone were displaced persons would be allowed back to their homes given the consent of the United Nations task force in Congo. Also on 31st British Foreign Minister David Miliband and French Foreign Minister Bernard Kouchner flew to the region with the intensions of stopping in Kinshasa, Goma, and possibly Kigali. On November 6th rebels broke the ceasefire again and wrested control of another town in eastern Congo clashing with government forces on the eve of the regional summit on the crisis. In November during the clashes around Goma a UN source reported that Angolan troops were seen taking part in combat operations alongside Congo government forces. Kinshasa repeatedly denied that foreign troops were on their soil, an assertion echoed by the UN mission which has 17 000 blue helmeted peacekeepers on the ground. Angola a former Portuguese Colony, sided with Kinshasa in the 1998-2003 Second Congo War that erupted when DRC was in a massive rebellion. In January 22$^{nd}$ 2009 the Rwandan military during joint operations with the Congolese army, captured Nkunda as he fled from the DRC into neighbouring Rwanda. Nkunda is currently being held at an undisclosed location in Rwanda. With the ending of the Joint Rwandan-DRC offensive against Hutu Militiamen responsible for the 1994 Rwanda Genocide. The Kivu Conflict has therefore effectively been ended on March 23$^{rd}$ 2009 the NCDP signed a peace treaty with the government, in which it agreed to become a political party in exchange for the release of its members. Over the weekend of 9$^{th}$ and 10$^{th}$ May 2009 FDLR rebels blamed for attacks on the villages of Ekingi and Busuruing in Congo's Eastern South Kivu province. More than 90 people were killed at Ekingi, including 60 civilians and 30 government troops, and dozens more were killed at Busurungi. The FDLR were blamed by the United Nations.

➤ Kwa-Zulu: A former national state of non-independent South Africa. A homeland in Natal Province in Eastern South Africa. It is situated close to the Indian Ocean between the Transkei and Durban. It ceased to exist in May 1994 following the first all-race elections in South Africa.

➤ Ladysmith Siege: The sieges of 1899-1900 one of the three sieges of the second Boer War, in which the Boer forces attempted to pen up their British opponents, and around which many of the actions of the war took place. An attempt to relieve the town was frustrated at the battle of Spion Kop (Jan 1900), but General Sir Redvers Buller (1839-1908) succeeded in the raising the siege on the 28$^{th}$ of February 1900.

➤ Lancaster House: The London venue which held various conferences preparing the way for Independence in several parts of the British Empire. It is most noted for the 1961 conference which paved the way to Kenyan Independence and the 1979 Conference in which the British Foreign Sectary, Lord Carrington managed to forge agreement to an Independence Constitution for Rhodesia (Zimbabwe) and for procedures to end the Civil War in the country.

➤ Late Period: In ancient Egyptian history this term refers to the period of the 25$^{th}$ to 30$^{th}$ Dynasties. The 25$^{th}$ Dynasty (Nubian) kings were devoted to the worship of Amun and stressed the importance of the position of the Divine Adoratice of the God at

Thebes. Royal princesses held the office, being appointed by the adoption. New buildings were erected and others restored both in Egypt and Nubia. The Dynasty ended with the invasion of the Assyrians in 671B.C. and 633B.C. Princesses loyal to Ashurbanial were installed in the Delta, with Thebes under the control of the Divine Adoratice. The Prince of Sais was strong enough to unite the country and set up the 26th Dynasty. There was an upsurge in artistic and cultural expression inspired by the best works of the Old Kingdom particularly Babylon which had overwhelmed Assyria and inevitably there was a clash with Egypt. The Persians invaded Egypt in 525B.C. and under the 27th Dynasty the country became a satrapy of the Persian Empire. From this time onwards, frequent revolt to gain independence are recorded in Greek sources following the ephemeral 28th and 29th Dynasties, the last native Kings formed the 30th Dynasty, but by 343B.C. Egypt was once more subjected to Persia until the conquest of Alexander III, the Great.

➤ Lebowa: A former state of non Independent South Africa, a black Homeland in Northern Transvaal Province North- East South Africa it was situated North East of Pretoria. It was granted self governing status in 1972. It ceased to exist in the May 1994 following the first all-race elections in South Africa.

➤ Lozi (Barotse) State: A State formed by a cluster of Bantu-speaking agricultural and cattle herding people of the western Zambia, living in the flood plains of the upper Zambezi. It was penetrated by hunters, traders and missionaries in the late 19th Century and under King Lewanika peacefully accepted colonial rule. During the Colonial period, the state was known as Barotseland and was controlled by Indirect Rule, so that their kingship and distinctive institutions survived.

➤ Libyan Crisis: The 2011 Libyan uprising began as series of protest and confrontations occurring in the North African state of Libya against Mummar Gaddafi's 42 year rule. The protestors began on 15th February 2011-03-15 and escalated into a widespread uprising by the end of February with fighting verging at the brink of civil war as of the 6th of March 2011. Slogans from the uprising in Tunisia and Egypt have been used connecting the Libyan uprising with the wider 2010-11 Middle East and North Africa protests. By the end of February Gaddafi had lost control of significant part of the country, including the major cities of Misurata and Benghazi. The Libyan opposition has since set up a National Transitional

Council and fee-press has begun to operate in Cyrenaica. Social media internet has played an important role in organising the opposition. Gaddafi remains in control of Tripoli, Sirt, Zliten and Sabha. Fighting is still continuing to day. Gaddafi remains in control of the well –armed Khamis Brigade among other loyalist military and police units and some believe a small number of foreign mercenaries. Some of Gaddafi officials as well as a number of current and retired military personnel have sided with the protestors and have requested outside help in bringing end to the massacres of non-combatants. Libya has finally been liberated from Gaddafi who is currently on there run from liberation fighter in August 2011.

➢ Liberia Civil War: Liberia has a unique history among African States and a special bond with the United States. The relationship between the two nation's stretches back nearing 200 years. In 1822 the American Colonization Society established Liberia as place to send freed slaves. African-American gradually migrated to the colony and became known as Americo-Liberians. Hence the country was named Liberia, which stands for 'Liberty". In 1847, the Americo-Liberian settlers declared the Independence of the Republic of Liberia. The Americo-Liberians established a nation that in many ways reflected the country the country they had left. Monrovia is named after the 5th American President James Monroe who sent aid to the freed slaves. The flag recalls the US flag with contrasting red and white stripes and Blue Square in the corner with a white star. The country's constitution and political structures were closely based on the American model; Liberia's bank note has been also modelled after the US dollar. The Americo-Liberians regarded Africa as the Promised Land but they did not integrate into the African Society. Once in Africa they referred to themselves as American and were recognised as such by the local Africans. In 1980 the government was reversed in a Military rebellion and from 1989 to 2003 Liberia witnessed two civil wars, the first Liberian Civil War 1989-1996 and the Second Liberian Civil War 1999-2003. These wars displaced hundreds of thousands of people and destroyed the country's economy. In 2006, a new administration was established with Ellen Johnson Sirleaf as President, however Liberia still copes with increasing challenges and rebuilding has been slow.

➢ Mahdi's Revolt: Mohammed Ahmad, the Mahdi of the Sudan joined the Samaniyya derivish order, but c1872 he proclaimed privately that he was al Madhi al Muntaza (The awaited or expected Madhi), who promised believers that a new order was imminent. He made a tour of the Sudan from Dongola to Sennar, from the Blue Nile to Kordofan, and convinced himself of the people's disaffection and discontent with the established order. In 1881 he made his first public appearance as Mahadi and Mahdism spread from Kordofan and Bahr-al-Ghazi to the Eastern Sudan, despite the dispatch of several fruitless and occasionally disastrous (as in the case of Hick Pasha) expedition against him. In 1884 he laid siege to Khartown and in 1885 the Governor-General Charles George (Chinese). Muhammad Ahmad died later in 1885 but the Sudan was to remain under Mahdist control until Kitchener reduced the Sudan in the following decade finally defeating the Mahdist at Omdurman.

➢ Mafeking Siege (Oct 1899-May 1900): The most celebrated siege of the second Boer War, during which Colonel Robert Baden-Powell and a detachment of British troops were besieged by the Boers. The news of their relief aroused public hysteria in Britain, the celebration being known as 'Mafficking'. The truth about the siege was rather different from the heroic action depicted by the British press. It is now known that the white garrison survived in the reasonable comfort as the result of the appropriating the rations of the Blacks, who faced either with starvation or with running the gauntlet of the Boers by escaping from the town.

➢ Maghrib (Maghreb): An area of the North-West Africa including the countries of Morocco, Algeria and Tunisia; largely occupied by Sedentary and Nomadic Berbers of the Kabyle, Shulh and Tuareg groups. In Arabic, the word refers to Morocco only.

➢ Maichew (Mai Cou): The Battle of 31st March 1936 was the decisive battle of the Italians invasion of Abyssinia, in which Emperor Haile Selassie was defeated and the Italian commander, Marshal Badoglio, prepared for the Italian camp at Maichew with forces which consisted of the Imperial Guard and large numbers of Galla under Feudal to repulse the Ethiopian Forces with superior artillery. It became Selassie's last despairing gesture before he fled into exile and the Italians were able to complete their conquest. Ethiopian resistance passed from the traditional leader to the guerrilla patriots.

➤ Maji Maji (1905): A rising against German rule which took place in Southern Tanganyika. People from a variety of ethnic backgrounds rose against harsh tax exactions and compulsory cotton growing. Priests and messengers moved from village to village urging people to rise and claiming that they had medicine which would turn bullets into water or maji. The German administration broke down for several months, but the rising was put down with great brutality causing a famine, in which a million people died, and a major ecological disaster in the region.

➤ Majuba Hill Battle (1881): An engagement which ended the first Boer War. In 1877 the British had attempted to federate the British and Boer territories of South Africa by invading and annexing the Transvaal. The latter was successfully accomplished, but the plan was destroyed by the British victory at Ulundi in the Zulu War of 1879. With the Zulu threat removed, the Boers resolved to re-establish their Independence. The British suffered several small reverses, culminating in their defeat at Majuba Hill. Gladstone's government then restored a limited independence to the Orange Free State and the Transvaal under the Pretoria Convention, subsequently modified by the London Convention of 1884. Disagreement about the interpretation of this Convention was to increase tensions later in the 19th Century.

➤ Malawi Congress Party (MCP): Founded in 1959, this part grew out of the Nyasaland African Congress. It was the only legal party in Malawi and had its life President Hastings Kamuzu Banda.

➤ Matabeleland: The name given to the region of Western and Southern Zimbabwe, between the Zambezi and Limpopo Rivers. It was named after the Matabele or Ndebele, an Nguni tribe related to the Zulu originally located in Natal and the Transvaal. Matabeleland was acquired by the British South Africa Company in 1893 it became part of Southern Rhodesia in 1923.

➤ Mau Mau: The phase used by the Colonial authorities for the uprising in Kenya, largely among the Kikuyu which caused a state of emergency in the early 1950's. Its aim were anti-colonial and anti-setter especially in formerly Kikuyu 'White Highlands' rather than self-consciously nationalist, and much of its violence was directed against fellow Kikuyu who were thought to be collaborating with the colonial authorities but the disruption id caused hastened the transition to Independence. However, very few of those who fought for the Mau Mau benefited materially from the transfer of power.

➤ Modder River Battle (1889): one of the engagements of the Second Boer War through which the British hoped to relieve the siege of Kimberly. The Boers had command of a hilltop, a traditional Boer tactic; but as this made them vulnerable to modern artillery, they gave up the hilltop and dug trenches by the river. The British failed to take the positions and were defeated two weeks later at Magersfontein, putting back the relief of Kimberly by three months.

➤ Movimento Popular de Liberatca de Angola (MPLA): Formed in 1975, under the leadership of Agostinho Neto, by the merger of several nationalist groups, the organisation faced opposition from UNITA and FNLA which could not be defused through negotiation after the ensuing civil war, the MPLA with its Cuban and Soviet allies formed the government in Angola, but faced with a continuing insurrection from UNITA with its South African and US allies. With neither side being able to prevail, negotiations took place and a cease fire was agreed in Estoril, Portugal in May 1991.

➤ National Party (NP): A political party formed in South Africa in 1912, to reflect the Boer (Afrikaner) interest. Over the years it absorbed smaller parties like the Afrikaner Party. It developed an explicit programme of Afrikaner advancement and separation of the races. It gained power in 1948 and retained power in South Africa and it then under F W De Klerk the party began to orchestrate the transfer of power from whites to a more democratic political base.

➤ Napata: An ancient city situated on the western bank of the Nile in what is now the Sudan. It was the capital of the Kingdom of Kush, c 750- 590 B.C. Although political dominance passed to Meroe in that year, Napata remained the Kingdoms religious capital.

➤ New Kingdom: In ancient Egyptian history the great era which began with the expulsion of the Hykos (c1567 B.C). This was when Egypt became an Imperial Power with a sphere of influence extending at its height, from the 4th Cataract of the Nile in the South to the Amanus Mountains of Anatolia in the North. The commitment of the early kings of the 18th Dynasty to a policy of expansion, with political control over Palestine and Syria, the exploitation of Nubia and the dedication of the spoils of war to Amun at Thebes as thanks offering for their victories, was continued by succeeding ruling families. In the reign of Amenhotpe III, the country reached the peak of its achievements culturally, economically and politically. Following the religious and artistic revolution of the Amarna period under Akhenaten (Amenhotp IV), the Ramesside Kings attempted to reimpose Egypt hold in Western Asia. However, the balance among the neighbouring nations began to shift away from economics based on bronze to those using iron. This combined with ethnic movements in the Mediterranean after 1200B.C. and the ever-increasing power of the priesthood of the Amun led to a steady decline in the Egypt's prestige and the end of the Empire in the early 11th Century Before Christ.

➤ Nkomati Accord: Essentially this was a non-aggression treaty signed between Mozambique and South Africa in 1984, in which Mozambique agreed not to support the ANC militarily. In practice, the superior power of South Africa meant that the agreement was implemented unilaterally.

➤ Northern African Campaign: A campaign fought during the World War II (1940-3) between Allied Forces and Axis Forces. After an initial Italian invasion of Egypt. Italian forces were driven back deep into Libya, and Rommel was sent to North Africa with the specially trained Afrika Corps to stem a further Italian retreat. The British were driven back to the Egyptian border, though they defended Tobruk. The counter-attack late in 1941 and fighting continued the following year, with Rommel once more gaining the initiative. In October 1942, British troops under Montgomery defeated Rommel at the Battle of El Alamein and drove the German troops west once more. In February 1943, the Germans attacked US troops in Tunisia were driven back and finally 250 000 Axis troops half of them Germans were caught in a pincer movement by Allied troops advancing from the East and West.

➤ Nguni Tribe: A group of Bantu-speaking people of the Southern Africa. They originally occupied present day Natal and Transkei. In the 19th Century they carried out a series of migrations. The main groups today include the Zulu, Swazi and Xhosa of South Africa and Swaziland, the Ndebele of Zimbabwe and the Ngoni of Zambia, Malawi and Tanzania.

➤ Nupe: An Islamic state in central Nigeria which resisted the encroachment of the Europeans in the 19th Century. It was conquered in1896 by Sir George Goldie and his forces of the Royal Niger Company. The Southern half of the Emirate was ceded to the British and a new emir was installed likely to be sympathetic to the company it was subsequently incorporated into the Colony of Nigeria.

➤ Nyamwezi Tribe: A group of people of the highlands of the North-Central Tanzania, south of Lake Victoria. In the 18th Century they created a trading network between the East African Coast and some of the states of Uganda. Later they extended their commercial influence to the Kazembe Kingdom in Zambia. Coastal Swahili and Europeans were in touch with them in the 19th century, particularly during the reign of their Chief Mirambo.

➤ Organisation Arme'e Secrete, Secret Army Organisation (OAS): The Clandestine organisation of French Algerians Led by rebel army General Jouhacid and Raoul Salaan, active 1960-2 in resisting Algeria independence. It caused considerable violence in Algeria and metropolitan France until thrown into rapid decline by the Franco-Algerian ceasefire in March 1962, Salaan's capture in April 1962 and the Algerian Independence July 1962.

➤ Omdurman Battle: An engagement outside Khartown in 1898, it confirmed the British reconquest of the Sudan. The British campaign under Kitchener had been authorised in 1895, and instituted with powerful Anglo-Egyptian forces in 1896. The overwhelming defeat of the massed forces of the Khalifa (the successor of the Mahdi), with many causalities illustrated the power of the modern weapons.

➤ Ogaden: The disputed region of Southern-Eastern Ethiopia which became part of Abyssinia in 1890 and part of Italian East Africa from 1936 to 1941. It is largely inhabited by Somali in the 1960's. The Somali invaded in1977, but were repulsed by Ethiopian Forces, fighting continued throughout the 1980's.

➤ Organisation of African Unity (OAU): An organisation founded in 1963 by representatives of the 32 African governments meeting in Addis Ababa, which reflected the views of moderate leaders such as Nyerere, rather than the radicals such as Nkrumah. By protecting territorial integrity the organisation accepted the artificial boundaries bequeathed by the Colonial powers and preserved individual self-interest over continental political and economic unity. It remained, however the main forum for the African Continent to express its political views and through its Liberation Committee in Dar es Salaam, assisted the decolonisation of Southern Africa. It has had some success at mediation but it lacked the power of Sanctioning has resulted in its inability to solve problems where major African powers disagree.

➤ Paardeberg Battle: The first major British victory of the Second Boer war 1900 following the relief of the siege of Kimberly. The Boers abandoned the position they had held at Magersfontein and moved east to defend Bloemfontein. Their defeat at Paardeburg opened Free State and the Transvaal, and the taking of the Boer cities.

➤ Pan Africanism: An ideal and a movement, drawing its ideas from Black Americans and West Indian writers and activitist. In part, it reflects a pride in the African continent and Africanism and thus has some similarities with negritude and in part, a commitment to self-rule. Although the pull towards continental unity is strong in rhetoric and emotional statements. Pan- Africanism has failed ultimately to provide rivalries nor has its political manifestation, the Organisation of African Unity, Managed to provide the Institutional framework for Continental Unity.

➤ Pan Africanist Congress (PAC): A South African political party and an offshoot of the African National Congress ANC. The PAC was formed in 1959 as a movement rejecting the multi-racial assumption of the ANC as well as its communists and Soviet links. It was banned in 1960 and its leaders went in to exile organising opposition to the Apartheid Regime in South Africa from Lusaka Zambia their ban was lifted in 1990. It remains smaller party compared to the ANC making it a closely knit party than the ANC, despite its having leadership problems in its early years in exile.

➤ Patriotic Front (PF): A Zimbabwean movement formed by the merging of the Zimbabwe African People Union led by Robert Mugabe and Zimbabwe African Peoples Union led by Joshua Nkomo in 1976, it was intended to unite  the major exiled nationalist movements in a concerted opposition, both political and military to Ian Smiths White minority regime. In the election held the under the Lancaster House Agreement in 1980 the PF won an overwhelming victory. In the post-independence period, however the front broke up when Nkomo whose principle power base was among the Ndebele people in Matabeleland and Mugabe who represented ZANU of the majority Shona people became estranged. Later they reconciled in a move by Mugabe to create a One Party State.

➤ Peoples National Congress (PNC): The major political party in Guyana, which has provided the government since 1964. Founded in 1955 by Forbes Burnham as a breakaway African party after a split in the Jagan's Peoples Progressive Party, it took Guyana to Independence in 1966 and has generally implemented socialist policies. Since Burnham's death in 1985, the PNC has retained power under the leadership of Desmond Hoyte.

➤ Pretoria Convention 1881: The agreement which brought to an end to the First Boer War, establishing Limited Independence for the Boer in Transvaal. In 1887 the secretary of state for the Colonies Lord Carnarvon and the High Commissioner in South Africa Sir Bartle Frere, resolved to attempt to reunite the two British Colonies and two Boer dates in Southern Africa. The Transvaal was invaded and annexed by Sir Theophilius Shepstone in an attempt to place its bankrupt finances on a second footing, but after the British suffered reverses in the Zulu war in 1879, the Boer set about re-establishing their Independence. The British were defeated at a number of small engagements in the Eastern Transvaal, notably Majuba Hill where the British Commander, General Sir George Colley, was killed. Gladstone's Cabinet resolved to abandon imperial responsibilities in return for a vague declaration of Suzerainty, under which the British would Control Boer Foreign policy. The Interpretation of the extent of such 'Suzerainty' beggared relations between British and Boer up to the Second Boer War of 1899-1902.

➤ Qwa Qwa: National state of the old South Africa it was a non-independent Black Homeland granted self governing status in 1974.

➤ Rassemblement Democratic Africaine (RDA): It was established in 1944, the RDA was a Cross-National Political Party with branches in most parts of the French African Empire, which sent members to the National Assembly in Paris. Its major figure was Felix Houphouet-Boigny.

➢ Resistencia Nacional Mozambicana (RENAMO): An armed movement set in 1976, first with Rhodesian and later South African support, to oppose the FERLIMO government of Mozambique, although lacking a clear political aim, it managed to disrupt Mozambique's economy and transport systems and was responsible for the pressurizing the government into signing the Nkomati Accord.

➢ Rhodesian Crisis: The series of events that began with the declaration of Unilateral Declaration of Independence (UDI) by Ian Smith on 11ᵗʰ November 1965, following the Rhodesian Government failure to agree with successive British Administration on a constitutional independence settlement that ensure the continuance of white supremacy. The British Government was successful in gaining UN support for sanctions while ruling out the use of force. In 1966 and 1968, Smith engaged with Prime Minister Harold Wilson in an ultimately unsuccessful attempt to resolve the crisis. An agreement was reached with Edward Heaths Conservative Government in 1971, but was ruled out after an independent fact finding mission determined that it would be unacceptable to the black majority. The growing influence of the African National Congress (ANC), and the withdrawal of the Portuguese from Angola and Mozambique served to remind Smith of his isolationism and in 1977 he announced that he was willing to enter into new talks on a one-man, one vote basis and released political nationalist leaders Ndabaningi Sithole and Joshua Nkomo as sign of good faith. However they initially refused to participate in negotiations and the escalation of terrorist activities continued unabated despite Smith having attained in 1978 an internal settlement, thus providing for multiracial government, with the moderate Sithole and Bishop Abel Muzorewa. The return of a Conservative Government in England in 1979 provided the springboard for fresh talks and a new settlement, leading to elections in 1980 that was won by ZANU PF and its former-Marxist guerrilla leader Robert Mugabe who still rules Zimbabwe today.

➢ Rhodesian Front (RF): The Rhodesian Political Party formed in 1962 to oppose the relatively United Federal Party, with Winston Field as its Leader. Ian Smith replaced him in a Putch in 1964. He later led the party and Rhodesia to its UDI. The RF had gained a majority of the seats in the 1962 general elections they sought out thereafter to preserve white dominance over the political and economic affairs of Rhodesia. In 1977 the pressure from the Civil War and outside international influential pressure. The party accepted the principle of universal adult suffrage and attempted to devise an internal settlement. They attempted to introduce a Government of National Unity by allowing Abel Muzorewa head the transition government in 1979. At the independence of 1980 the RF changed its name to the Conservative Alliance of Zimbabwe.

➢ Royal Niger Company: A company founded to secure the Niger region for the British traders amalgamated on the River Niger into the formation of the National African Company, which in 1886 obtained a Royal Charter to rule a large part of what later became Nigeria. They secured the navigable portions of the Niger which surely frustrated the French and destroyed their power of African Middlemen. The Charter was wound up in 1888 and he various parts of Nigeria were later amalgamated as a British Colony, which achieved its Independence in 1960.

➢ Rwandan Genocide: Was the 1994 mass murder of an estimated 800 000 people in the small East African nation of Rwanda. Over the course of approximately 100 days from the assassination of Juve`nal Habyarimana on April 6th it culminated from a long standing ethnic competition and tensions between the minority Tutsi who had controlled power for centuries and the majority Hutu people who had come to power in the rebellion of 1959-62 and overthrew the Tutsi Monarchy. In 1990, the Rwandan Patriotic Front (RPF) composed of Tutsi refugees, invaded Rwanda from Uganda in an attempt to defeat the Hutu-led government. This began the Rwandan Civil War fought between the Hutu regime with support from France and the RPF with support from Uganda.

➢ Segu: A West African State founded (c1650) by the Bambara, a Mande- speaking agricultural people. They also formed the state of Kaarta (Mali) c 1753-4.

➢ Senegambia: Confederation of the association between the Gambia and Senegal, begun in 1982, designed to integrate military, economic, communications and foreign policies. They set out to establish joint institutions, while preserving independence and sovereignty. It proved to be limited in value and was ended by mutual agreement in 1989. Though I feel it was a base of the unification of the African Continent and should be used as a pilot example to the total unification of Africa.

- Sharpeville Massacre: 21 March 1960 at the Police Station in South African Township of Sharpeville in the Transvaal Province (Gauteng). After a day of demonstrations, at which a crowd of black protestors far out numbered the police, the South African Police opened fire on the crowed, killing 69 people. Some sources state that the crowed were peaceful, others sources state that the crowed had been hurling stones at the police injuring several police officers, and the shooting only started when the crowed advancing toward the fence around the Police station. Since the 1920's, the movement of black South Africans were restricted by pass laws leading up to the Sharpeville Uprising, the Apartheid supporting National Party government under the leadership of Hendrik Verwoerd used the pass laws to enforce greater segregation and in 1959-1960 extended them to include women. The African National Congress (ANC) had decided to launch a campaign of protests against the pass laws. These protests were to begin on the 31st March 1960, but the rival Pan Africanist Congress (PAC) decided to pre-empt the ANC by launching it own campaign ten days before on 21 March. On 21st March between 5000 and 7000 people converged on the local police station in the township of Sharpeville near Johannesburg offering themselves up for arrest for not carrying their pass books. This was part of broader campaign organised by the PAC.

- Six Day War: (5-10 June 1967): Arab-Israeli War in which President Gamal Abd al-Nasser of Egypt blocked the Tiran Straits to Israeli shipping and massed troops in the Sinai Peninsula, while King Hussein allowed Iraqi forces into Jordan. Taking pre-emptive action, Israel paralysed the Egyptian air force and with response to the Jordanians move and the Syrian attacks they captured East Jerusalem, the West Bank, Golan Heights and Sinai. Israel unexpected victory was achieved in six days. Afterwards Arab States have since refused to negotiate any peace with Israel which has therefore held on to the so-called 'Occupied Territories' expect for Sinai which was returned to Egypt after the Peace Agreement of 1979.

- Slave Trade: A trade of Africans which started in ancient times. Slaves were sent across the Sahara and were traded in the Mediterranean by Phoenicians Giraeco-Roman traders in the Red Sea and beyond who traded slaves from East Africa to Egypt and the Middle East. These traders continued in medieval times, but the scale of the trade built up with the arrival of the Portuguese in

Africa and the development of the labour intensive plantations system in the West African Island of Sao Tome and Principe, Brazil, the Caribbean, the Southern American Colonies, and later the Indian Ocean Islands and South and East Africa. The Portuguese dominated the trade in the 16$^{th}$ Century; the Dutch in the early 17$^{th}$ Century, while the late 17$^{th}$ Century was a period of intense competition came from the French, British, Danes and Swedes. The Trade reached its peak in the second half of the 18$^{th}$ Century and from this period of Omani power up to the 1860's. The British abolished the Slave Trade in 1807, and the institution of Slavery in 1833. They then instituted their Royal Naval Anti-Slavery Squadrons on the coast of the Western and Eastern Africa. There have since been estimates of the number of salves removed from Africa, there most reliable figure being 12.5 million between 1650 and 1850. Many other people must have lost their lives in the Wars stimulated by the trade, and the total drain meant that at the very least the African population remained static for over two centuries. The abolishment was firstly implemented by the British Empire by an Act of parliament of 1807. The Society for Effecting the Abolition of the Slave Trade was founded in 1787 and was spearheaded by the 'Clapham Sect or Saints', whose membership included Ramsay, Clarkson, Stephen and Fowell Buxton and which was found a political voice in William Wilberforce the MP for Yorkshire. Although the Wilberforce's abolition bill first lacked government support during the Pitt administration. In 1806 the Tories we replaced by the Whigs of Charles James Fox, who made the Bill Law a year later. Kitty Amelia a British Slave Trader from Liverpool left in May 1808. The USA also abolished the Slave Trade in 1808. Denmark had abolished it 1804, France in 1818 and Spain in 1820.

> Songhai: A West African State which rose to power in the region formerly dominated by Mali in the Second half of the 15$^{th}$ Century, commanding the trade routes of the Sahara, the great market at Timbuktu, and the area Westwards to Senegal. It declined as a result of the Portuguese re-orientation of the trades routes, and was attacked by Moroccan forces in the 1590's. Songhai people still control much of the Saharan caravan trade.

> South Africa Act (1909): The Act of the British parliament which created the Union of South Africa from the British Colonies of the Cape of Good Hope; Orange River Colony and the Transvaal Colony. The Act made the provision for admitting Rhodesia as a

fifth province of the Union in the future but Rhodesian colonist rejected this option in a referendum held in 1902. The South Africa Act 1909 was the third major piece of legislation passed by the parliament of the Untied Kingdom with the intent of uniting various British Colonies and granting them some degree of autonomy.

➢ Southern African Development Coordination Conference (SADCC): An association of 10 African States Angola; Botswana; Lesotho; Malawi; Mozambique; Namibia; Swaziland; Tanzania; Zambia; and Zimbabwe with its headquarters in Gaborone. Its first meeting was held in Arusha in 1979 and its Lusaka Declaration of April 1980 set forth a commitment to a peaceful transition in Apartheid South Africa. SADCC was intended to aid the member countries to limit their dependency on trade with South Africa. It proved to be sectoral coordination and acted as a conduit for international aid to the region.

➢ SOWETO Riots (April-June 1976): These were the Soweto Students disturbances which took place in the township of the Transvaal called the South Western Townships (SOWETO), when several hundreds of students were killed resisting the teaching of the Afrikaans in schools. The township has remained a source of tension and violence in the New South Africa to date.

➢ Spion Kop Battle (1900): A battle of the second Boer War which was part of the British attempt to relieve the siege of Ladysmith, a town in Natal besieged by the Boers since October 1899. The British attempted to take a hill a few miles from the town and although they were close to success at one stage, the Boers succeeded in beating them off. There were 1500 British causalities, and together with the reverse at Vaal Krantz in the same week, it continued the succession of the defeats which the British suffered during the early months of the War.

➢ Sudan People's Liberation Movement (SPLM): they proclamation of an Islamic State in the Sudan in 1977 by their Leader Numayri who led the unrest in the South which saw the emergence of the SPLM, this movement initially represented a political refusal to accept the dictatorship of the government in Khartoum and they eventually moved to an armed rebellion under Colonel John Gurang.

➤ Suez Crisis (1956): A political crisis focused on the Suez Canal. Intensive rearmament by the Egypt. The Egyptian nationalisation of the Suez Canal, and the establishment of a command with Jordan and Syria aimed at surrounding and eliminating Israel in Sinai, following this attack, the British and France asked both sides to withdraw from the Canal Zone and agree to the Israel temporary occupation. When this was rejected by Egypt, the British and France invaded, but withdrew following diplomatic action by the USA and the USSR. Israel was also forced to relinquish the Sinai Peninsula back to Egypt. They were allegations of collusion between Israel, France and the British over the matter.

➤ Swahili: A language spoken in East Africa, especially in Tanzania it's a hybrid of Arabic and local languages, it also has provided a bridge across tribal dialect divides and has been seen by a many as a national and region language of East Africa.

➤ South West Africa People's Organisation (SWAPO): Founded in 1958 as the movement for South-West Africa (Namibia) became the main nationalist movement for Namibia and organised the Guerrilla War against the South Africans administration of the country. They were based initially in Tanzania and then Zambia, the guerrilla movement established bases in Angola in the 1970's and became embroiled in the general conflict involving South Africa, UNITA and the MPLA government in Luanda with its Cuban and Soviet support. They were recognised by the OAU and later the World Community as the authentic voice in Geneva in 1988 which was linked to Namibia's Independence after the Cuban withdrawal from Angola and the cessation of the South Africa support of UNITA. In the ensuing of the 1989 elections SAWPO won over half the votes and majority seats to form the first Independent government.

➤ Tanganyika African National Union (TANU): this party was founded in 1954, grew out of the Tanganyika African Association and was dominant party in Tanganyika during the period leading to independence Under the leadership of Julius Nyerere, it became first de facto the only party in the country and then in 1966, de jure only party. Noted for internal competition it provided at election time and for it unique brand of Socialist Ideology, laid out in the Arusha Declaration, the party merged in 1977 with the Afro-Shirazi Party of Zanzibar to form Chama Cha Mapinduzi (CCM).

➤ Tobruk Battles (1941-2): The Libyan port of Tobruk, 50 miles from the Egyptian Frontier was captured from the Italians by British Forces on 22 January 1941. Axis Forces under Rommel subsequently defeated the British, but it was decided to hold Tobruk. The siege of Tobruk began on 10th April 1941, and the port was relieved by the British on 10th December 1941. Tobruk was subsequently captured by Rommel on 21 June 1942 and finally retaken by the British following the battle of El Alamein in November 1942.

➤ Tunisian Revolution: was an intensive campaign of civil resistance, including a series of street-demonstrations taking place in Tunisia. The event began in December 2010 and led to the ousting of long time President Zine El Abidine Ben Ali in January 2011. Street demonstration was precipitated by high unemployment, food inflation, corruption and lack of freedom of speech and other political freedoms and poor living conditions. The protests constituted the most dramatic wave of social and political unrest in Tunisia in three decades resulting in scores of deaths in Tunisia.

➤ Tripolitania: A region of the North Africa, laying between Tunis and Cyrenacia a former province of western Libya; under Turkish control from the 16th Century until the Italians control until 1943;it was under British control until 1952.

➤ Unilateral Declaration of Independence (UDI): This Act was by the Rhodesian government declaring independence from The Untied Kingdom. It was signed on the 11th November 1965 by the administration of Ian Smith Rhodesian Front Party opposed to black majority rule in the then British Colony. Although it declared Independence from the United Kingdom it maintained allegiance to Queen Elizabeth II. The British Government; The Commonwealth and the United Nations condemned the move as illegal. Rhodesia reverted to defacto and de jure British control as 'The British Dependency of Southern Rhodesia for a brief period in 1979 to 1980, before regaining its independence as Zimbabwe in 1980.

➤ Uganda Martyrs- A group of 22 African youths converted to Roman Catholicism in 1885-1887, they were killed for their faith in Uganda by the reigning King Mutesa II of Buganda. They were canonized in 1964.

- Ujama: A Swahili word usually translated as 'family hood' which is applied to the special brand of African Socialism espoused by Julius Nyerere of Tanzania. It emphasizes on co-operation and equality was based upon the conception of the traditional African society.

- Umkhonto We Sizwe: The military wing of the ANC literally translated 'Spear of the Nation'. It was established when the ANC was banned its main bases were based in Angola, Tanzania and Zambia. It Chief of Staff in the 1980's was Joe Slovo. It provided a number of new generations of the leaders such as Chris Hani who was assassinated in 1995? In South Africa.

- United National Independence Party (UNIP): Formed in 1959 with Kenneth Kaunda as the Leader, UNIP was the strong party in the Last years of Northern Rhodesian Colonial rule and provided the first Independence government of Zambia. It became the only legal party in 1972 but in 1991, after pressure from the international community and widespread sign of the dissatisfaction within the country, multiparty elections were held and UNIP was convincingly defeated Chiluba's party Movement for Democratic Change MDC of Zambia.

- Uniado Nacional para a Independecia Total de Angola (UNITA): Which is the National Union for Total Independence of Angola is an Angolan nationalist party founded in 1966 by Jonas Savimbi. Its support was based in South Eastern Angola and even after Angola gained Independence from Portugal in 1975 it waged a guerrilla war against the MPLA government. It received backing from the USA and South Africa. When the Civil War seemed to have reached an inconclusive position of stalemate, after long and a difficult negotiations UNITA and MPLA agreed upon a ceasefire in Estoril in early 1991.

- United Gold Coast Convention (UGCC): The political party founded in 1947, which was led originally by Dr J B Danguah. It was first organisation to seek self-governing of Ghana within a short time frame. For a while its General-Secretary was Kwame Nkrumah, he broke away to form the more radical Convention Peoples Party (CCP) which defeated UGCC in the 1951 elections after which UGCC was dissolved.

> Urabi Revolt (1881-2): A demonstration in Egypt, led by Colonel Ahmad Urabi Pasha, an Officer of the Egyptian Army from peasant origin. It forced the Khedive to accept a nationalist government. Urabi was initially an Under-Secretary and subsequently became Minister of War. The revolt was in essence a reaction of Junior Officers of Native Egyptian origin against the Turko-Girrassions who tended to monopolise the senior ranks of the Army. Unfortunately for Urabi, these developments occasioned disquiet among the British and French, who demanded that the Khedive dismissed the Nationalist Government? This dismissal provoked xenophobic disorder and Urabi prepared to face the possibility of direct British and French intervention. The British eventually moved against Urabi destroying the defences of Alexandria he had prepared and defending the Egyptian Army at Tel el-Kebir.

> Volksraad: The ruling council of the Boer Republics in South Africa Volksrands were established by the various Boer communities in the interior of Southern Africa after the Great Trek which commenced in 1835. They became the legislative bodies of the Transvaal and the Orange Free State up to the Boer War of 1899-1902. Volksraads were also created by the Grigua or Half-Caste Republics established on the Frontier of the Cape in the 19th Century.

> Voortrekkers: The Boer migrants who left the Cape Colony from 1835 onwards to escape the British Rule and create Independent Republics in the interior of Southern Africa. The British took the Cape during the Napoleonic Wars and held it after the peace settlement at Vienna. New land owning systems, legal and administrative concepts, the English language with British settlers and more missionary activity were all introduced under their rule. The Boers took particular exception to the new legal status of their black workers, they emancipation of Slaves in 1833 and the inability of the British to introduce acceptable frontier policies. A number of columns of Voortrekkers left under a series of leaders including Louis Tregardt, Piet Retief, Gerrit Maritz and Hendrik Potgieter. About 6000 Boers left the Colony and established small republics in regions across the Orange Free State, Transvaal and Natal. Many withdrew from Natal when it was declared a British Colony in 1843. For the rest of the 19th Century, the British made repeated and largely unavailing attempts to bring them back within their jurisdiction. The Voortrekkers were commemorated by a powerful and romantic Monument in Pretoria.

➢ WAFD Party: The name of the Egyptian Nationalist Party which sent a delegation under the nationalist leader Sa'd Zaghlul to the High Commissioner in 1919; the word means 'delegation'. The Wafd Party became Egypt's official opposition party in 1984, but was replaced as such in 1987 by an alliance headed by the Muslim Brotherhood.

➢ WARS in Africa: There are currently fifteen African countries involved in war or are experiencing post-war conflict and tension. In Western Africa countries include Cote d'Ivoire, Liberia, Nigeria, Sierra Leone and Togo; In Eastern Africa countries include Eritrea, Ethiopia, Somalia, Sudan, and Uganda. In Central Africa countries include Burundi, Democratic Republic of Congo, and Rwanda. In North Africa the countries include Libya and Algeria. In Southern Africa countries include Angola and Zimbabwe. The base of these wars is the rich natural resources each of these poor countries holds in timber, oil, and diamonds compounded in many cases by the foreign extractive industries presence, their opaque, unreported payments to the governments and the governments opaque unreported use of money to create and fund wars. The wars serve the purpose of creating a distraction as the countries and their fleeing citizens are robbed of their countries natural resources easily converted to cash, for the personal use and the fortunes of the ruling parties. Tribal conflict is deliberately antagonised so it can be blamed for the conflict.

➢ Witwatersrand (Gauteng): the region literally meaning the Whiter Waters Reef centred on a ridge of the Gold-bearing rock in Southern Transvaal a province of the Old South Africa now called Gauteng. Johannesburg is a city in Gauteng it became the power house of the South African economy, with a lot of Black township surrounding it providing a reserve of labour. Gold was discovered in 1886 and then it became the largest Gold producer producing over half the worlds gold supplies.

➢ Yaba Higher College: A college founded in Lagos, Nigeria in 1934 by the British Governor General, Sir Donald Cameron, with the intention of training Africans for administrative work, it offered degree courses after World War II.

➢ Yoruba City States: A cluster of politically autonomous units in Nigeria and Benin inhabited by the Kwa-speaking people and each ruled by a King who is both political and religious head. The dominant state in the 17th and 18th Century was the Kingdom of Oyo, which broke up the early 19th Century. Ibadan was the largest pre-colonial city in Black Africa, and the states are famed their art. Missionaries were highly active in Yoruba Land in the 19th Century by Islam and traditional religions where also represented.

**PART THREE:** A-Z of African Nationalist Liberation Leaders and their actions which made African history, this part is aimed at giving the reader an insight into each individual's leadership in their different Liberation movements. It names the African Presidents; Prime Ministers; Military Leaders and the Dictators who led their countries into Independence and on how their countries managed internal rivalry, coups and general politics.

➢ Abbas, Ferhat (1899-1955) Algerian Nationalist Leader, he founded the Muslim Student's Association in 1924, before becoming a Chemist. He served as volunteer in the French army in 1939, but after France's defeat he produced in 1942 a 'Manifesto of the Algerian Peoples'. In 1955 he joined the Front de Liberation Nationale (FLN), the main Algerian resistance organisation and worked with Ben Bella in Cairg, before founding a Provisional Government of the Algerian Republic in Tunis. After Independence in 1962, he was appointed President of the National Constituents Assembly but he fell out of favour and was exiled. He was rehabilitated shortly before his death.

➢ Abboud, Ibrahim (1900-83): A Sudanese Solider, he was the Commander-In-Chief of the Sudanese army from the time of Independence in 1956. He was the Military Regime leader of Sudan which obtained power when Abdullah Khalil surrendered the reins of government to the army in 1958. Abboud's regime was unable either, politically or economically to maintain effective rule over the country, and was overthrown in 1964. Abboud himself resigned and retired into private life.

➢ Aguiyi, Ironsi Johnson (1925-66): Nigerian Solider and Politician. He joined the colonial army in 1942 and was trained in the UK before commanding the Nigerian contingent in the UN involvement in the Congo (Zaire). Appointed Commander-In-Chief in 1965, he assumed power following the Officers Coup of January 1966, but was killed in the counter-coup led by Gowon Yakubu in July 1966.

➢ Ahadjo, Ahmadou (1924-89): Cameroonian Politician educated at the Ecole Superieure d'Administration, Yaoundé, he was a radio operator in the post office before entering politics in 1947, being elected to the territorial Assembly. He represented Cameroon in the Assembly of the French Union 1953-7. From 1957 to 1960 he held a senior position in the Territorial Assembly of Cameroon. In 1960 when most of the French Cameroons was amalgamated with the

British Cameroons, he became President and was re-elected to the post in 1972, 1975 and 1980. He resigned in 1982 and went into voluntary exile in France. His one-party state, although severe on the rivals whom he outlawed was relatively successful economically and less repressive than many West African States.

➢ Afrifa, Akwasi A (1936-79): He was a Ghanaian Solider and Politician who were educated at Adisadel College. He joined the Colonial army in 1956. He trained at Sand Hurst England and twice served with the United Nations Army in the Congo (Zaire). He was part of the group that overthrew Kwame Nkrumah in 1966 and became a member of the National Liberation Council and thus he assumed Military Leadership of Ghana. He handed power over to civilian rule in 1969, but when the Military intervened again in 1972 he was detained for a while. When the Military handed over to another civilian rule period he was tried and executed for corrupt practices.

➢ Aguiyi-Ironsi, Johnson (1925-66): Nigerian Solider and Politician. He joined the colonial army in 1942 and was trained in the United Kingdom before commanding the Nigerian contingent in the UN involvement in the Congo (Zaire). He was appointed Commander-In-Chief in 1965, he assumed power following the officers' coup of January 1966, but was killed in the counter coup led by Gowon Yakubu in July 1966.

➢ Ahmadu, Ibn Hammadu (c1775-1844): West African Islamic leader. He was influenced by the example of the Usman dan Fadio in Northern Nigeria; he led a Jihad or Holy War in the western Sudan. It started about 1818 and made Ahmadu master of a state of some 50 000 square miles, including within its borders the important centres of Jenne and Timbuktu. In 1862 it was conquered by another leader of a Jihad, al-Hajj Umar ibnTal.

➢ Amer, Abd Al Hakin (d 1967): Egyptian Solider and Politician, was one of the nine officers who after meeting in the Aftermath of the disastrous 1948 war, formed the original constituent committee of the Free Officers Movement in 1949. In 1950 Gamal abd al-Nasser was elected Chairman of this Committee and, when he became Prime Minister in 1954, it was Amer this time a General who took over as War Minister. In 1967, following the Six Day War, Amer now Filed Marshal and disillusioned by what he saw Nasser's betrayal of the army, allegedly to part in a conspiracy against him.

Arrested for his supposed part in his plot, Amer was arrested and subjected to a campaign of humiliation by the press. He committed suicide while in custody.

➤ Amin, Idi (Dada) (1925- ): Ugandan Soldier and President. He joined the Kings African Rifles in 1946, fought with the British Army in the Kenyan Mau Mau uprising and was heavyweight Boxing champion of Uganda. He benefited from the rapid Africanisation of the army after Uganda Independence in 1961 and was promoted to Major General in 1968. He seized power from President Obote in January 1971, dissolved parliament and proclaimed himself President. During his Presidency, there was widespread violence in Uganda, a mass expulsion of all Asians and the massacring of his opponents especially from the Langi and Acholi tribes. He was deposed by exiled Ugandans with the help of Tanzanian army in 1979, he fled to Libya and thence he went to Saudi Arabia (1980-8). After a brief sojourn in Zaire, he returned to the Arab world.

➤ Azhari, Ismail Al (1900-69): Sudanese Politician he was the leader of the Sudanese Unionist Party which to the surprise and indeed disappointment of the British was the victor of the Sudanese Parliamentary elections in 1953. Al Azhari formed the first government in 1954.

➤ Azikiwe, Nnamdi (1904- ): Nigerian Journalist and Politician. He spent four years as a government clerk before going to the USA, where he studied at Storer College, Lincoln University and Howard University. He then taught at Lincoln, where he obtained two further degrees. He returned to Africa in 1934 and edited the African Morning Post in Accra before going back to Nigeria to take up the editorship of the West African Pilot in 1937. He was member of the executive of the Nigerian Youth Movement (1934-41) and helped found the National Council of Nigeria and the Cameroons (NCNC) of which he became Secretary between 1944-46 and then President 1947-60. A member of the Nigerian Legco in 1947-51, he became Premier of the Eastern Region in 1954 after two years as the leader of the opposition. He was appointed the first black Governor-General of Nigeria in 1960 and he became the first Nigerian Republic's President in 1963 to 1966. He was in Britain at the time of the 1966 military coup, but returned as a private citizen soon afterwards. He returned to politics in 1979 as leader of and successful candidate for the Nigerian Peoples Party. He became a member of the Council of State 1979-83.

➢ Babanginda, Ibrahim (1941- ): He was a Nigerian Solider and Politician educated at military schools in Nigeria and later in India, the UK and the USA. He was commissioned in 1963 and became an instructor at the Nigerian Defence Academy. During the Nigerian Civil War, he commanded an infantry battalion, and then became an instructor for the Nigerian Defence Academy from 1970-2 and later commander of the Armoured Corps 1975-81. He was involved in the military coup of President Shagari in 1983; he became a member of the Supreme Military Council and Chief of Staff in 1985 and was the leader of the coup which overthrew Muhammadu Buhari in 1985. He was responsible for the cautious and controlled was of Nigeria returning to civilian rule. He imposed a two-party system and staged elections in Nigeria.

➢ Banda, Hastings Kamuzu (1905- ): He was a Medical Doctor and Politician. He left Malawi by foot for South Africa, from where he later travelled to the USA and Britain to obtain medical qualifications. He set up practice in Liverpool and then in Tyneside before moving to London, where he became deeply involved in opposition to the Central African Federation, but after a scandal involving his liaison with a white woman, he went to Ghana, from where he was persuaded to return to Malawi to lead the Nyasaland African Congress there. He was jailed in 1959 but was soon released and was appointed the Minister of National Resources and Local Government (1961-3), Prime Minister of Nyasaland (1963-4) and then of Independent Malawi (1964-6). When the country became a Republic, he became its first President and then proclaimed himself as Life President of the Malawi Congress Party and Malawi from 1971, he retained many portfolios, notably Defence, through out his period as President he depended on a mix of populism, a functioning political party and a ruthless use of his security apparatus, he became and survived as the dominant figure in Malawi politics for over 30 years. (?)

➢ Barreto, Francisco de (1520-73): Portuguese Military Commander. He attempted an ambitious conquest of the Zambezi Valley, the Mashonaland plateau and the Kingdom of Mwene Mutapa in 1572. In 1575 a treaty was concluded between the Portuguese and the Mwene Mutapa king whereby Muslims would be expelled and the Portuguese be allowed to trade, to seek gold and conduct missionary work. The Portuguese maintained trading footholds in the interior of what is now Zimbabwe until expelled in the 1690's.

➢ Ben Ali, Zinel Abidine (1936- ): Tunisian Politician, after studying electronics at military school in France and the USA, he began a career in military security rising to the position of the Director-General of National Security. He became Minister of the interior and then Prime Minister under President for life Habib Bourguiba, who had been in power since 1956. In 1987 he forced Bourguiba to retire and assumed the presidency and immediately embarked on constitutional reforms, promising a greater degree of democracy.

➢ Biko, Steve (Stephen) (1947-77): South African Black Activist, he studied medicine at Natal University from whereby he became President of the all black South African Student Organisation (SASO) in 1969 and honorary President of the Black Peoples Convention in 1972. He was the major figure in the Black Consciousness Movement and his challenge to Apartheid, expressed in his organisation of the Black Community Programme, led to his banning and the detainment. He died in police custody as a result the torture he received.

➢ Biya, Paul (1933- ): Cameroonian Politician, he graduated with Law degree from Paris University and entered politics under aegis of Ahmadou Ahidjo. He became a junior minister in 1962, a minister of state in 1968 and the Prime Minister in 1975. When Ahmadou Ahidjo unexpectedly retired in 1982, he became the President and he reconstituted the government with his own supporters. He survived a coup attempt in April 1984 supposedly instigated by Ahidjo. He was re-elected President of Cameroon in 1988 with more than 98 percent of the vote.

➢ Bludell, Sir Michael (1907-93): Kenyan Farmer and Politician born in London. He immigrated to Kenya in 1925 to farm, and served in the army during World War II. He then involved himself in settlers politics, he became a member of the Legco from 1948-63 and leader of the European members from 1952-4. He then was appointed Minister of Agriculture 1955-9 and 1961-3. He broke off with the dominant white minority group to exposé political change involving the majority black Kenyans in national politics and was then much vilified for this by the whites. However, he was an essential bridge between the white dominated Colonial years and the black majority rule of Independent Kenya.

➤ Blyden, Edward Wilmot (1832-1912): Western Indian Writer and Educational Philosopher. He spent most of his life in West Africa and is generally as one of the founders of the concept of negritude and the precursors of the intellectual and political nationalism of Africa of the 20th century. Blyden believed in the establishment of a vast Colony under British rule in West Africa as the means whereby the Continent could modern itself. Such a Colony would aspire to Dominion status and then be ruled by its own elite fully educated in the western ways but also re-discovering its own essential African characteristics. At one stage he favoured Christian missionary endeavour as a means of reaching this goal, but later turned increasingly to traditional beliefs and Islam. He wrote many books and articles on these issues and worked for the foundation of a West African University.

➤ Bokassa, Jean Bedel (1921- ): Central African Soldier and Politician. He was educated in mission schools before joining the French army in 1929. He rose through the ranks and after independence, was made Army Commander-In-Chief, with the rank of Colonel. On 1st January 1966 he led coup which overthrew President Dacko and then he steadily entrenched his power, first by making himself life President; then in 1976 he modelled himself on Napoleon by crowning himself Emperor of the renamed Central African Empire. His rule was noted for its gratuitous violence and in September 1979 he was driven from the country and went into exile first in the Ivory Coast and then into France. He was sentenced to death in absentia. However, in 1986 he was returned for trial and found guilty of murder and other crimes, he was sentenced to life imprisonment.

➤ Botha, Louis (1862-1919): South African Politician and Solider. Born in Greytown, Natal, he was a member of the Transvaal Volksraad and commanded the Boer forces during the Boer war. In 1907 he became Prime Minister of the Transvaal Colony, and subsequently became the first Prime Minister of the New Union of South Africa from 1910-19. He suppressed De Wets rebellion in 1914, and then he conquered the German South-West Africa (Namibia) 1914-15. He died in Pretoria.

➢ Botha, Pieter Willem (1916- ): South African Politician. The son on internee in the Anglo-Boer War, he was steeped in politics. His early life lacked success he dropped out of University but he found his metier as a party organiser. With his confidence and courage, he was a formidable operator. He was an Advocate of Apartheid before the National Party gained power, he entered Parliament in 1948 and became Deputy Minister of the Interior (1958-61). Minister of Community Development, Public Works and Coloured Affairs (1961-66), Minister of Defence (1966-78) and Prime Minister (1978-89). Leader of the Cape section of the National Party. In 1966 he was chosen as leader of the Party when John Balthazar Johannes Vorster resigned. He won on a second ballot only because the Transvaal Nationalist was divided. He thus then became Prime Minster. Having built up the defence forces and supported the invasion of Angola in 1975, he now sought constitutional changes, but his ideas were too progressive for some of his Party some members defected in 1982 to form the Conservative Party, which were too cautious to appeal to the Black opposition. He suffered a stroke in 1989 and resigned a year later.

➢ Buhari, Muhammadu (1942-) Nigerian Solider and Politician educated locally and then at Military Academies in Nigeria, England and India, he became Military Governor of the North-Eastern State from 1975-6, then of Bornu State in 1976, then was appointed the Federal Commissioner of Petroleum Resources from 1976-8 and then to become the Chairman of the Nigerian National Petroleum Corporation 1976-9. He returned to the army duties in July 1976. He led the military coup which ousted Shedu Shagri 31st December 1983, and made himself President. He was removed in a coup led by Ibrahim Babangida on the 27th August 1985.

➢ Burnham Forbes (1923-85): Guyanese Politician, he was educated in Britain. Burnham represented the African element in the Guyanese population and was co-leader with Cheddi Jagan of the Multiracial People's Progressive Party until 1955. In that year he split with Jagan over the latter's support for International Communism and set up a rival African-based Party, The People's National Congress (PNC). The PNC slowly gained adherents in Jagans troubled years after 1961 and in 1964 Burnham became Prime Minister he negotiated an Independence Constitution in 1966 and in 1970 established Guyana as a Cooperative Socialist Republic remaining its President until his death in 1985.

➢ Busia, Kofi (1913-78): Ghanaian academic and politician. Educated in Kumasi and at Achimota College, he then obtained an external BA degree London and a PHD in Philosophy from Oxford. He was one of the first Africans to be appointed an Administrative Officer in the Gold Coast (Ghana). He resigned that position to become a lecture and later Professor of Sociology at the University College of Ghana. He was elected to Legco in 1951, became a leader of the National Liberation Movement (1954-9) in opposition to Kwame Nkrumah. He went into exile (1959-66), taking up the Chair of Sociology at Leiden University. After the 1966 coup, he returned as adviser to the National Liberation Council and then founded and led the Progress Party which won the 1969 election. He became Prime Minister (1969-72) before being overthrown in another coup, going into exile again in 1972. He held various Academic posts and died in Oxford.

➢ Buthelezi, Chief Mongosuthu Gatsha (1928- ): South African Politician and Zulu Chief Leader. Expelled from Fort Hare University College in 1950, where he was a member of the African National Congress (ANC), he was a government interpreter in the Native Affairs Department (1951-7). Officially appointed as Chief of the Buthelezi tribe in 1957, he was also an assistant to the Zulu King Cyprian 1953-68 before being elected leader of the Zulu Territory Authority in 1970 and Chief Minister of Kwa-Zulu in 1976, with the ANC's approval. He was sympathetic to the ANC's opposition to Apartheid and he rejected the Boer South African plan to turn Zululand into a Bantustan or Homeland but increasingly he became inclined to work within the Apartheid System. He later founded the Inkatha Freedom Party of which he is still President. He held a number of Ministerial posts one of which was that of Home Affairs Minister under the New South African Parliament of the ANC led by Nelson Mandela.

➢ Cabral, Amilcar (1924-73): Guinean Nationalist Leader. He was educated at Lisbon University; he worked as an Agronomist and Agricultural engineer for the Colonial Authorities. He founded the PAIGC ( ) in 1956 and, after abortive constitutional discussions with the Portuguese Government he initiated a Revolutionary war in 1963. Noted for his commitment to politicising the peasantry and establishing alternative institutions in liberated territories, he presided over successful war which forced the Portuguese to concede Independence. He was murdered in 1973 just as his aim was being achieved.

➢ Cabral, Luiz (1931- ): Guinean Nationalist Leader, he is brothers with Amilcar, he was educated in Portuguese Guinea and became clerk and trade union organiser. As a member of the PAIGC, he went in to exile in 1960 and took part in the guerrilla struggle to win Independence for Guinea Bissau; success made him President of the New Republic of Guinea Bissau 1974-80, he was overthrown in Coup in 1980.

➢ Chidzero, Bernard Thomas G (1927- ): Zimbabwean Politician and United Nations Administrator. He was educated in Southern Rhodesia and Marianhill in South Africa; he went to Pius XIII Catholic College (Lesotho); Ottawa University (USA) and then Nuffield College, Oxford (England) from where he graduated with a Dr Phil in 1960. He was successively assistant research Officer Economic Commission for Africa in Addis Abba (1961-3); Representative of the United Nations Technical Assistance Board in Kenya 1963-6; Resident Representative UNDP (1966-8), Kenya; Director of Commodities Division UNCTAD (?) 1968-77 and then Deputy President General 1977-80. He was elected to the Zimbabwe Senate (1980). He became Minister of Economic Planning and Development in Zimbabwe until his death in? Although he was not a member of the Politburo, he has been the Chief Architect of Zimbabwean's economic policy and the leading figure among reformists who prevailed over the radicals wish for a more Socialist and Leninist State.

➢ Chilembwe, John (1871-1915): He was Nyasaland (Malawi) religious and military leader. After receiving his education in the USA, he returned to Nyasaland where he established his Providence Industrial Mission, an independent African Church and Mission in 1906. He became increasingly discontented with white rule and petitioned for black rights in various areas. When his appeals were ignored, in 1915 he led a rising against the British, through which he hoped to replace the White Rule by divine assistance. Two Europeans were killed, but the revolt was suppressed and Chilembwe was killed while trying to escape. It was the first major act of Black Resistance in Malawi, and he became an inspiration to subsequent African Nationalism.

➤ Chissano, Joaquin (1939- ): Mozambique Politician, he graduated from high school in Maputo and then he went to Portugal to study Medicine, where he became involved in political activity. He was founder member of FRELIMO and became the head of its Department of Security and Defence. A close confident of Samora Machel, he became Foreign Minister after Independence in 1975, he was responsible for the negotiating of the Nkomati Accord with South Africa. He succeeded Machel in 1986 and began the process of change inside Mozambique.

➤ Dacko, David (1930-): Central African Politician educated at a Teachers Training College in Mouyoundzi, He became a teacher and then trade unionist before being elected to the Territorial Assembly in 1957, becoming successfully Minister of Agriculture (1957-8); Minister of Administrative Affairs (1958); Minister of the Interior (1958-9) and then Prime Minister (1959-60). He became the first President of the Central African Republic (1960) but was deposed in a coup, led by Bokassa, in 1966 and was imprisoned until 1976 when he was appointed Bokass's advisor. With the aid from the French he was responsible for removing Bokassa in 1979, becoming President, a post to which he was re-elected in 1981, but then was removed from Office by a military coup led by Andre-Dieudonne Kolingba.

➤ Danquash, Joseph Boakye (1895-1965): He was a Ghanaian nationalist and politician. After pursuing his studies in London, where he qualified as a Lawyer. He returned to Ghana and founded the Times of West Africa in 1931. He was a leader of the United Gold Coast Convention (UGCC), which campaigned for Independence, but he fell out with Nkrumah Kwame who formed the Convention Peoples Party in 1949 who won the elections. He was imprisoned in 1961-2 and 1964-5 he died in prison

➤ Dioria, Hamani (1916-87): Niger Politician, he was educated in Dahomey and then at the William Ponty School in Dakar. He became a Teacher and then an Instructor in the Language School for Colonial Administrators (1938-46); he helped form the Rassemlement Democartique African in 1946 and represented Niger in the French Assembly (1946-51) and (1956-7). In 1956 he became Prime Minister of Niger and in 1960, at Independence, its first President. Building on their close relations with France, he ran on of the most stable countries in West Africa, being re-elected in 1965 and 1970, but opposition within his Party the Niger Progress

Party (NPP) led to him being overthrown in April 1974 through a Military Coup. He was placed under house arrest for 13 years, before he left for Morocco where he died.

> Diouf, Abdu (1935- ): Senegalese Politician, he studied in Dakar and Paris University where he graduated with a Law Degree. He returned to Senegal to work as a Civil Servant. After holding a number of posts, including that of Secretary General to President Leopold Sedor Senghor, he became Prime Minister in 1970, and succeeded Senghor on his retirement 1st January 1981. He was re-elected President of Senegal in 1983 and 1988.

> Doe, Samuel Kenyon (1951-90): Liberian Solider and Politician, he joined the army as a private in 1969, reaching the rank of Sergeant in 1975. In April 1980 he led a coup of Junior Officers in which President Tolbert was killed. In 1981 he made himself General and Army Commander-In-Chief. He established a Political Party the National Democratic Party of Liberia in 1984 under whose aegis he narrowly won the 1985 Presidential election. Widespread dissatisfaction with his rule generated several opposition groups and a virtual Civil War erupted in 1989, which the Economic Community of West African States (ECOWAS) attempted to mediate, Doe was killed in the ensuing internal struggle for power in 1990.

> Dos Santos, Jose Edurado (1942- ): Angolan Nationalist and Politician, he joined the Movimento Popular de Liberation de Angola (MPLA) in 1961 and was forced into exile in Zaire, where he founded the MPLA Youth League. In 1963 he went to the USSR to study Petroleum Engineering and Telecommunications and then to Lisbon to study Medicine. He returned to Angola in 1970 to participate in the Liberation War. He was responsible for the MPLA's medical services. He being a close confident of Agostinto Neto, he became Foreign Minister on Independence and First Deputy Prime Minister, Planning Commission. When Neto died in 1970 he succeeded the Presidency. He was conscious of the fighting UNITA with its South African backers was destroying Angola, he negotiated the withdrawal of his Cuban backers and the 278 South African UNITA backers in 1989 ensuing a ceasefire between MPLA and UNITA ?.

- Eyadema, Etienne Grassingbe (1937- ): Togolese Soldier and Politician, he joined the French army in 1953, serving outside Africa for many years. He became Togo's Army Chief of Staff in 1965. He led a bloodless Military Coup in 1967, deposing President Grunitsky? He banned all Political Parties until 1969, when he founded a new organisation, the Rassemblement du Peuple Togolias, as a vehicle for the organisation to support for the government. Despite opposition he managed to survive and he also responded by a degree of Democratization.

- Fanon, Frantz (1925-61): Martinique born Doctor and Revolutionary. His study of the Algerian revolution. The Wretched of the Earth which he wrote in 1961 became the inspiration and manifesto for their Liberation Struggles throughout the Third World. Educated as a Psychiatrist in France was sent to Algeria, Fanon changed sides and joined the rebels but died of leukaemia before seeing the achievement of the Independence of Algeria.

- Gaddafi, Muammar (1942- ): Libyan Political and Military leader. He abandoned his university studies in the favour of military training in 1963 and went on to form the Free Officers Movement which overthrew King Idris in 1969. He became Chairman of the Revolutionary Command Council, he then promoted himself to Colonel and then he became the Commander-In-Chief of the Libyan Armed Forces. As de facto head of state, he set about eradicating Colonialism by expelling foreigners and closing British and USA bases. He also encouraged a religious revival and returned to the fundamental principles of Islam. Gaddafi is known to be somewhat an unpredictable figure; he has openly supported violent revolutionaries' in other parts of the world while he also ruthlessly pursued Libyan dissidents at home and abroad. He also ruthlessly pursued Libyan dissidents at home and abroad. He also waged war in Chad, he threatened his other neighbours. In the 1980's Libya and his palaces and other territories were bombed and Libya aircrafts where shot down by the Americans. He is now has an uprising against his rule and is currently engaged in battles all over Libya against rebels.

- Garang, Colonel John (1943- ): Sudanese Solider, he studied agricultural economics in the USA, he returned to Sudan, where he joined the army. He went back to the USA for Military Training, which was followed by a post at the Military Research Centre in Khartoum. In 1983 he formed the Sudanese People's Liberation

Movement in the Southern Sudan were being exploited by the country's Northerners, Waging a relentless guerrilla campaign, the organisation has posed a considerable threat to the stability of the Sudan. Involving conflict with the regular Sudanese army, the movement's activities have done much to increase the sufferings of the peoples in a country already racked by famine.

➤ Gouled, Aptidon Hassen (1916- ): A Djiboutian Politician while serving as a representative of the French Somiland in France. He became increasingly involved in the activity for the Independence Movement of Somali and in 1976. He founded the African People's League for Independence (APLI). Djibouti achieved self-government in 1977 and he became the country's first President, later merging the APLI with other political groups to form the country's only Political Party the 'People Progress Party'. His policy of neutralism in a war-torn region of the African Continent ensured his continuing popularity and in 1987 he was re-elected for a final six-year term.

➤ Gowon, Yakubu (1934- ): Nigerian Solider and Politician. A Christian in a Muslim area, he was educated at CMS missionary School and then at the Government College Zaria. His military training began in Ghana and continued in the UK where he attended the Royal Military Academy, Sandhurst, among other institutions. He was commissioned into the Nigerian Army in 1956, serving with the UN force in the Congo (Zaire) in 1960-1. He became Adjutant-General in 1963 and Chief of Staff in 1966. The ethnic conflicts in country precipitated a coup on 15th January 1966 led by Ibo Officers; Gowon headed a counter-coup in July 1966. He then became Head of the Federal Military Government and Commander-In-Chief. Unable to prevent a Civil War he fought to retain Biafra (The Eastern Region) within a single Nigeria, while acceding to ethnic concerns by increasing number of States; with the assistance of both the USA and the USSR, he prevailed. However, his retarded return to Democracy encouraged another Military Coup he was deposed in 1975 and fled into exile.

➤ Graaf, Sir de Villers (1913-79): South African politician, he was educated in South Africa, the UK and the Netherland. He served in the World War II. He was elected as a United Party Member of Parliament in 1948; he became Party Leader in 1956, remaining so until so until 1977, when he transferred his allegiance to the New Republic Party. The political heir to Jan Smuts, his opposition to the National Party was too gentlemanly to challenge its hegemony and too conservative to build a new coalition across the race divide. He epitomized the failure well-meaning Liberalism in these years.

> Habre, Hissene (1930- ): Chadian Nationalist Politician, he was the son of a Desert Shepherd, he worked as a clerk for the French Army before becoming an Administrator. He joined FAN? Guerrilla in the early 1970's but having made his peace with President Malloun in 1978, he was appointed Prime Minister. When Goakouni seized power himself in 1982. When Goukouni seized power in 1979, he became Defence Minister. However, supported by the CIA, he fought against Goukouni and took power himself in 1982 with French Military assistance and support from African Heads of State, he forced Libya withdraw from Northern Chad. He uneasily retained power?

> Habyarimana, Juvenal (1937- ): Rwandan Solider and Politician. He was educated at a Military School; he joined the National Guard and rose rapidly to the rank of Major-General and Head of the Guard by 1973. In the same year?, as fighting between the Hutu and Tutsi tribes restarted he led a bloodless coup against President Gregoire Kayibanda and established a Military Revolutionary Development Movement (MRND) as the only legal party and promised an eventual return to constitutional government.

> Haykal, Muhammad Hasanayn (1924- ): Egyptian Journalist and Author. Early in his career he covered the 1948 War and the Korean War. He had contacts with the Free Officers before the 1952 Coup, and his subsequent career has spanned the period from Gamal Abd al-Nasser's Presidency to the period in office of Hosni Mubarak who period was toppled by a peoples uprising January/February 2011. He became the most influential journalist of his generation; Haykal became Editor of the respected Cairo Newspaper al-Ahram in 1957, writing on subjects such as Nasser's relationships with World Leaders such as Nikita Khrushchev and Lyndon B Johnson, in addition to other Arab Heads of States. He also had contacts with Guerrilla Leaders, including Che Guevara. He was removed from the Editorship of the al-Ahram in 1974 following his criticism Anwar Sadat's conduct of the October War, Haykal was briefly held under arrest in 1981 when Sadat ostensibly to deal with the religious extremism of the Muslim Brotherhood, Sadat extended his purge to include Journalist and Opposition Party Leaders.

- Hertzog, James Barry Munnik (1866-1942): South African Politician. He was a Boer General (1899-1902) and in 1910 he became Minister of Justice in the first Union Government. In 1913 he founded the National Party, advocating complete South African Independence from Britain. As Premier, in the coalition Government with Labour (1924-9) and with Smuts in an Untied Party (1933-9), he pursued a legislative programme which destroyed the African franchise on South Africa. He created jobs reservation for whites, and also tightened land segregation. He renounced his earlier secessionism, but at the outbreak of World War II he declared for neutrality and he was defeated he retired in 1940.

- Hofmeyr, Jan Hendrik (1845-1909): South African Politician, he took Journalism as 'Onze Jan', he rose to be the political leader of Cape Dutch and dominated the Afrikaner Bond. He represented the Cape at the Colonial Conferences of 1887 and 1894. After the Jameson Raid (1895) he parted from Rhodes, and thereafter worked outside parliament, his Nephew Jan Hendrik (1894-1948), became Deputy Premier to Jan Smuts and advocated a Liberal policy towards the black Africans.

- Horton, James Africanus (1835-83): Sierra Leonean Doctor and Surgeon- Major. He served in the British Army and was the Author of the West African Countries and Peoples in 1868. He acted as an adviser to the Traditional Chiefs in the Gold Coast, and is regarded as on of the intellectual founders of modern West African Nationalism.

- Houphouet-Boigny, Felix (1905-93): Ivorian Politician. The son of a Chief, he was educated in Cote d'Ivorie and at Dakar and then became a Medical Assistant and Planter before turning to Politics. He was appointed President of the Syndicat Agricale Africain in 1994 and was founder of the Parti Democartique de la Cote d'Ivoire (PDCI). He was elected to the French Constituent Assembly 1946-58, he held a series of Ministerial Posts. He became Prime Minister of the Cote d'Ivorie in 1959 and then President at their Independence in 1960. His paternalistic rule, which also combined close relations with France and his support for Capitalistic rule, support he gained from capitalistic enterprises saw Cote d'Ivoire initially develop more successfully compared to most West African Countries. The building of palace and a Cathedral at Yamoussoukro reduced his popularity and profligacy of economic decline.

- Hoyte, Hugh Desmond (1929- ): Guyanese Politician, after studies at the London University and the Middle Temple, he taught in boy's school in Granada (1955-7) and then practised a Lawyer in Guyana. He joined the Socialist People's Congress Party (PNC) and in 1968, two years after Guyana achieved full independence was elected to the National Assembly. He held a number of Ministerial Posts before becoming Prime Minister under Forbes Burnham. On Burnham's death in 1985, he became President.

- Huggins, Godfery Martin 1st Viscount of Rhodesia and Bexley (1839-1971): Rhodesian Politician, born in England he immigrated to Southern Rhodesia in 1911 as a Doctor but was soon drawn into politics, being elected at the first after internal self-government. He was catapulted into the Premiership of Southern Rhodesia (Zimbabwe; Zambia and Malawi today) of which he was one of the Chief Architect. He retired in 1956, although the Central African Federation proved short lived and with Huggins readiness to respond to African Nationalist pressures became too limited, he then established a Liberal base in Southern Rhodesia (Zimbabwe) where class was deemed more significant than race. The combined forces of African Nationalism and White reactions squeezed Liberals into weaker positions of no power in the 1960', but the development of the State of Zimbabwe's Politicians inherited owes a great deal to Godfrey Huggins leadership during the difficult World Economic conditions in the 1930's; 1940's and 1950's.

- Jagan, Cheddi (1918- ): Guyanese Socialist Politician and Writer. With Burnham, he led the Nationalist People's Progressive Party (PPP) in demanding self-government in the early 1950's. The Jagan-Burnham alliance won the 1953 elections but the Governor, accusing Jagan of Communist Policies suspended the constitution, dismissed Jagan and his Cabinet and called in British troops. His acme to power again with the PPP in 1957, with an austerity of budget from the Imperial rulers. His desire to hasten the end of Imperial Rule led to racial rioting and long general strike in Georgetown which only ended by further British Military intervention (1961-4). In 1964 elections, based on a British –devised proportional representation constitution, when Burnham's People's National Congress was victories and Jagan became the leader of the Official Opposition.

➤ Jawara, Alhaji Sir Dawda Kairabi (1924- ): Gambian Politician, he was educated at a Muslim Primary School, Methodist Boys High School Bathurst and Achimota College in Ghana. He studied Veterinary at Glasgow and Edinburgh Universities. He returned to the Gambia as Veterinary Officer (1954-60), before entering Politics as Leader of the People's Progressive Party, becoming Minister of Education 1960-2 and then Prime Minister at Independence in 1963. On Gambia becoming a Republic in 1970 he became its first President. He was re-elected in 1972; 1977; 1983; and 1987 despite an abortive coup against him in 1981, which was put down by Senegalese troops and which paved the way for the formation of the short lived Confederation of Senegal and Gambia as Senegambia.

➤ Jonathan, Chief Joseph Lebua (1914- ): Lesotho Chief and Politician, he was educated in Mission Schools before working in South African mines and then in the local government of Basutoland, he entered politics in 1952 he joined the Basutoland National Council in 1956 and in 1959 founded the Basutoland National Party, which favoured a free enterprise economy and cordial relations with South Africa. He was elected to the Legco in 1960, he then went to become Prime Minister in 1965, and he went on to suspend the Constitution in 1970. Parliamentary Governance was restored in 1973 and elections were held regularly until 1985, when they were cancelled. Chief Jonathan was overthrown in a Military Coup in January 1986.

➤ Joubert, Petrus Jacobus Piet (1834-1900): Boer Soldier and Politician, born in the Congo and grew up in the Cape Colony. He fought against the British in the Transvaal (1880-1), and became Vice-President under Stephanus Johannes Paulus Kruger (1883). He led the first Boer successes of the Boer War 1899-1902, but died in Pretoria after a short illness.

➤ Kadalie, Clements (1895-1951): Born in Malawi, he became a Trade Union Leader in 1919 in Cape Town South Africa. He formed the Industrial and Commercial Workers Union of South Africa, the first large-scale trade union for black people. He led a series of dock strikes in the Cape. By 1923 it had become a mass a movement reaching a peak of membership of 86 000 in 1928. However it declined rapidly from1929 onwards and was defunct by 1933, failing because Kadalie led it into Political action, it split into Moderate and Radical factions. He expelled the Communists and this forced the creation of a separate organisation in Natal. It also never secured a large membership among the workforce of the Rand Gold Mines and also failed to gain international recognition.

> Kapwepwe, Simon (1922-89): Zambian Nationalist Leader and Politician. Educated in Mission Schools before becoming a teacher. He went on to help found the Northern Rhodesian African National Congress in 1946. After a period of study in India, he returned to be Treasurer and then helped form the breakaway United National Independence Party (UNIP) of which he became the Treasurer 1960-7. After holding several Ministerial Posts in the early days of Independence, including the Vice-Presidency. He resigned from UNIP to form the United Progress Party (UPP) in 1971 in order to oppose UNIP led by Kenneth Kaunda. The UPP was banned in 1972, when Zambia became a One-Party State. Kapwepwe was detained he later rejoined the UNIP in 1977.

> Karume, Sheikh Abeid (1905-72): Zanzibari Politician, he was a Sailor, he became active in local politics in the 1940's was elected as town councillor in 1954 and helped found the Afro-Shirazi Party in 1957. Following the 1964 which deposed the Sultan of Zanzibar, he became the President of the Revolutionary Council. When Zanzibar united with Tanganyika in 1964 to form Tanzania, He became Vice-President, but after he expressed opposition to democratic changes made him enemies and he was assassinated in 1972.

> Kasavubu, Joseph (1910-69): Zairian Politician, he was educated locally in a Seminary School. He worked as a Teacher and then a Civil Servant in the Belgian Colonial Administration before entering Politics. He became Mayor of Leopoldville in 1957 and with the support of the United Nations he struggled for power against Patrice Lumumba to become the President of the Congo in 1960.

> Kaunda, Kenneth David (1924- ): Zambian Nationalist Leader and Politician, he was educated in Mission Schools and Munali Secondary School, he became a Teacher and Welfare Officer before entering politics and becoming the Secretary-General of the Northern Rhodesian African National Congress in 1953, a breakaway from it to form the Zambian African National Congress in 1958. After a spell in prison as a result of his Nationalist activities, he took over from Mainza Chona as leader of the United

independence Party (UNIP) in 1960, he was appointed Minister of Local Government and Social Welfare (1962-3) in the first all black African Government. He then went on to become President on Independence in 1964. He was a close friend of Julius Nyerere and followed his version of African Socialism called Humanism. He eventually made Zambia a One Party State by making UNIP the sole legitimate party which made Zambia decline economically due to his political Liberalism. He faced pressure from democratic movements from around the world and within his country. He called an election in 1991 and was defeated by Chiluba's Movement for Democratic Change (MDC).

➢ Kawawa, Rashidi Mafume (1929- ): Tanzanian Trade unionist Nationalist Leader and Politician. From an early age he was involved in Labour Politics, becoming President of the Tanganyika Federation of Labour. From 1957 he was a member of the Tanganyika Legislative Council and when Julius Nyerere resigned as Prime Minister in 1962, Kawawa briefly replaced him, He became the First Vive President (1962-4) and was re-elected after the amalgamation of Tanganyika and Zanzibar in 1972 he was once again appointed Prime Minister. As a result of his overly zealous commitment to the Tanganyika African National Union. Guidelines set forth in the Arusha Declaration; he was demoted to Minister of Defence and National Service in 1977, but returned to the Office of the President in 1980. He lost status in the government of Mwinyi who replaced Nyerere, but he was re-elected almost unanimously as Secretary-General of the Chama Cha Mapinduzi (CCM) in the 1987 congress?

➢ Keita, Modibo (1915-77): Mali Politician educated at William Ponty School, Dakar. He helped to found the Rassemblement Democrdique Africaline in 1946 and was elected to the Territorial Assembly in 1948. He was a Deputy in the French Assembly 1956-9 before becoming President of Mali (1960-8). He was a radical who looked to Kwame Nkrumah for Leadership. He was overthrown by the Military in 1968 and was imprisoned until death.

➢ Kenyatta, Jomo Kamou Ngengi (1891-1978): Kenyan Nationalist and Politician. Educated by Scottish Missionaries, he joined the Young Kikuyu Association in 1922 and Politics thereafter dominated his life. He edited the Kikuyu Central Associations News Sheet, Mwigwithania, which played a major role in representing progressive black Kenyan opinion in the 1930's. He visited London on numerous occasions to lobby government. He also visited the USSR several times and learnt and met most of the Anti-Colonial Lobbyist in the United Kingdom, where he worked through out the World War II. He attended the famous fifth Pan-Africanist Conference in Manchester (1945) and on his return to Kenya in 1946; he was elected President of the Kenyan African Union, becoming the country's major spokesman for the Anti-Colonial Movement. On the out break of the Mau Mau uprising and the subsequent emergency, he was tried, found guilty on what later proved to be perjured evidence and was detained until 1961. Chosen in absentia to be the President of the Kenyan African National Union in 1960, he was elected to the Legco in 1962 and then after the Independence elections became Prime Minister in 1963 and then President when Kenya became a Republic in 1964. A remarkable mixture of Kikuyu Nationalist, pragmatic politician and father-figure he was popularly known as 'Mzee' or 'Oldman'. He surprised observers by leading Kenya into a period of economic growth and unexpected tribal harmony.

➢ Kerekou, Mathieu Ahmed (1933- ): Benin Soldier and Politician. The son of a Soldier, he joined the Colonial Army, being trained in France whose army he served. He joined the Dahomey Army at Independence in the 1961, rising to command it in 1966. He took part in the 1967 Coup which overthrew President Soglo but returned to the Army, while remaining the Vice- President of the Military Revolutionary Council (CNR). In 1972 he led a further Coup, establishing a National Council of Revolution and espousing 'Scientific Socialism'. He renamed Dahomey Benin and began to return the country to democracy, being first elected to the Presidency in 1980 and re-elected in 1984 and 1989. He dissolved the (CNR) and finally resigned from the army in 1987 as a gesture of his commitment to Democracy.

➢ Kitchener of Khartoum and of Broome, Horatio Herbert, 1st Earl (1850-1916): A British Field Marshal and Statesman. He joined the Royal Engineers in 1871, and served in Palestine (1874), Cyprus (1878), and the Sudan (1883). By the final route of the Khalifa of Omdurman (1898), he won back the Sudan for Egypt, and was made a peer. Successively he was the Chief of Staff and Commander-In-Chief in South Africa 1900-2, he brought the Boer War to an end and was made Viscount. He then became Commander-In-Chief in India (1902-9), Counsel-General in Egypt (1911), and Secretary for War (1914), for which he organised manpower and a vast scale (Kitchener Armies). He was lost with the HMS Hampshire, mined off the Orkney Islands.

> Kruger, Stephanus Johannes Paulus (Oom uncle) Paul (1825-1904): Afrikaner Politician, he took part in the Great Trek of the 1930's, becoming leader of the Independence Movement when Britain annexed Transvaal (1877). In the first Boer War (1881) he was head of the Provisional Government and subsequently became President of South Africa Republic (1883-1902). During the Boer War 1899-1902, he came to Europe to seek in vain alliances against the British. He made his headquarters at Utrecht. He died at Clarens, Switzerland.

> Lenshina, Alice (): The Leader of the Millenarian Movement, of the Lumpa Church which led opposition in 1964 to the newly Independent regime in Zambia. The church and its followers represented the split between modernisers and traditionalist. Lenshina's Church became a major focus of opposition to the regime of Kenneth Kaunda.

> Limann, Hilla (1934- ): Ghanaian Diplomat and Politician, he was educated in Ghana and then at the LSE and then the Sorbonne, where he earned a Doctorate. He was a teacher be fore joining the Ghanaian Diplomatic Service as Head of Chancery at Lome (1968-71). Limann then served his country at many international gatherings while being his country's counsellor at its permanent mission to the Untied Nations in Geneva (1971-5) and a Senior Officer in the Ministry of Foreign Affairs (1975-9). In 1979 he was chosen to lead the Peoples National Party and was its successful Presidential candidate in the 1979 elections, becoming President until his removal from Office on the 31st December 1981 as a result of a Coup led by Flt-Lt Jerry Rawlings.

> Lumumba, Patrice, Hemery (1925-61): Congolese (Zairian) Politician. He was educated in Mission Schools, both Catholic and Protestant. He became a Post Office Clerk and then Director of the Brewery. He helped form the Movement National Congolias (MNC) in 1958 to challenge Belgium Rule and when the Congo was granted Independence he was made its first Prime Minister in 1960. He became a symbolic figure in African History as he sought to unify the Congo and opposed the secession of Katanga under Moise Tshombe. He was arrested by his own Army in September 1960 and was handed over to the Katangese and murdered. His

name however remains significant as the embodiment of African Nationalism and the opponent of balkanization manipulation by ex-Colonial Countries and their Allies.

➢ Luthuli, Albert John Mvumbi (1898-1967): South African Nationalist. He qualified as a teacher and taught for 15 years before succeeding to the Chieftainship of Groutville, the community in Natal in which in which he had been raised, in 1935. He joined the ANC in 1946, became President of the Natal branch and led a campaign of passive resistance against Apartheid, for which he was deposed from his Chieftainship by the South African Government. He became President of the ANC in 1952, reflecting the colour-blind traditions of the Party, but was repeatedly 'Banned', and was imprisoned (1956-7). He was awarded the Nobel Peace Prize in 1966.

➢ Luwum, Juani (1922-77): Ugandan Bishop, the son of a Christian. He became a teacher and was converted in 1948. He was ordained into the Anglican Church and despite his evangelicalism which disturbed more conventional Christians in Uganda. He became a Theological College Principal and then the Bishop of Northern Uganda and was then elected Archbishop of Uganda in 1974. He spoke out fearlessly against the atrocities committed during Idi Amin's period of rule, as a result of which he was murdered. So concerned was the Amin Government that a memorial service for him was forbidden.

➢ Machel, Somora Mosies (1933-86): Mozambique Nationalist Leader and Politician. He trained as a Medical assistant before he joined FRELIMO in 1963, which soon became a Guerrilla force that fought against the Portuguese Colonial power. He became the Commander-In-Chief in 1966; he succeeded Mondlane Eduardo after his assassination in 1969 by a parcel bomb in Dar es Salaam (Tanzania). Avowedly a Marxist, his success at politicizing the peasants in Northern Mozambique during the Liberation War Led him to believe in his dominant role in the Party after the flight of the Portuguese in 1974. He became the first President of Mozambique from its Independence in 1975. His economic failures due to his policies, he became more pragmatic, turning to the West for assistance, and also advising Robert Mugabe to be temper principled with prudence, he then began to establish a more harmonious relationship with Apartheid South Africa. He was killed in an air crash after attending the Nkomati Accord meeting with Apartheid South Africa.

➢ Malan, Daniel Francois (1874-1959): South African Politician, he was educated at Stellenbosch and Utrecht Universities, in 1905 he joined the Ministry of the Dutch Reformed Church but in 1915 left to become editor of the Die Burger, the Nationalist Newspaper. He was an elected Member of Parliament in 1918; he held the portfolios of Minister of Interior; Education; and Public Health by 1924. He helped reform the National Party to its decisive electoral victory in 1948 and oversaw the initial implementation of the policy of Apartheid he retired in 1954.

➢ Mandela, Nelson Rohlihlahla (1918- ): South African Nationalist Leader and Politician. He was educated at Fort Hare College (1938-40); He practised Law in Johannesburg before joining the African National Congress (ANC) in 1944. He founded the ANC Youth League. He was banned from 1956-61 and then arrested and sentenced to life imprisonment in 1964 for the leadership of the ANC, he spent most of the next 25 years in prison on Robben Island only being released on President F. W. De klerk's orders on 11th February 1990. He was elected the Deputy President of the ANC by the Party in exile in April 1990 and in April 1991 he was elected President. In 1993 he was jointly awarded the Nobel Peace Prize with F W De Klerk, and in 1994 he became South Africa's First Black President.

➢ Margai, Albert Michael Sir (1910-80): Sierra Leone Politician, the son of a Trader and the brother of Sir Milton Margai. He was educated in Roman Catholic Schools before becoming a Nurse and Pharmacist. He studied Law in London (1944-7) and was elected a member of the Legco in 1951, when he was appointed Minister of Education, Welfare and Local Government. A member of the Sierra Leone People's Party from 1951-8, he then helped to found the People's National Party and became Minister of Finance at Independence. When his brother died, he succeeded him as party leader and Prime Minister (1964-7). Following a Coup which was led by Siaka Stevens in 1967 he went into exile in London.

➢ Margai, Milton (1895-1964): Sierra Leone Nationalist Leader and Politician. The elder brother Sir Albert Margai, he was educated in Roman Catholic Mission Schools, Fourah Bay College and in the United Kingdom, where he qualified as a Doctor. Appointed a member of the Protectorate Assembly in 1940, he was elected to the Legco in 1951, when he helped to found the Sierra Leone People's Party and played a major role in pressing for Independence he became the first Prime Minister of Sierra Leone until his death in 1964.

➢ Masire, Quett Ketumile Joni (1925- ): Botswana Journalist and Politician. As a Journalist, he was the Director of the African Echo in 1958. He helped in the founding of the Botswana Democratic Party with Sir Seretse Khama in 1962 becoming it Secretary-General. He was appointed Deputy Prime Minister in 1965; he became Minister of Finance in 1966 and Vice President 1966-80 when Botswana became a Republic. He then took over the Presidency on Sir Seretse Khama's death in 1980.

➢ M'ba Leon (1902-67): Gabon Politician, he was educated in Catholic Schools; he in turn became an Accountant, a Journalist and Administrator. He was elected for the Rassemblement Democratique Africaine to the Gabon Assembly in 1952 and the French tradition, used the Mayoral position of Libreville to enhance his Political ambitions. He was Head of Government 1957-60 and President from Gabon's Independence until his death in 1967.

➢ Mboya, Thomas Joseph (1930-69): Kenyan Trade Unionist and Politician. Educated at Catholic Mission Schools and Ruskin College Oxford. He was an employee of the Nairobi City Council when he became Treasurer of the Kenyan African Union in 1953. He was elected Secretary-General of the Kenyan Federation of Labour in 1955 and a member of the Legco in 1957. He was the founder member and Secretary-General of the Kenyan African National Union (KANU) (1960-9). His reformist instincts brought him into conflict with his fellow Lou Oginga Odinga but he eventually won over Oginga Odinga forcing him out of KANU after the Party's Conference at Limuru in 1966, thus binding himself closer to Jomo Kenyatta. He became Minister of Labour (1962-3), and then Minister of Justice and Constitutional Affairs (1963-4). He then was appointed Minister for Economic Planning and Development (1964-9) where he implemented his essentially Fabians Philosophy in reformist socialism establishing the Free Enterprise within state regulations economic system which Kenya still epitomizes. He was assassinated in 1969.

➢ Mengistu, Hiale Mariam (1941- ): Ethiopian Solider and Politician, he trained at Guenet Military Academy and then firstly to part in the attempted Coup against Haile Selassie in 1960, he was not put on trial for that, he was instead appointed a member of the Armed Forces Co-ordinating committee (Dergue) which helped overthrow Haile Selassie in 1974. He then manipulated himself into the Chairmanship on the Dergue and became its undisputed Leader and Head of State in 1977. He allied himself with the USSR and modelled himself upon Cuba's Fidel Castro; he sought a socialist transformation for Ethiopia while retaining its territorial borders intact. Mismanagement, drought and internal War weakened his hold on the country. He eventually fled from Addis Ababa on 21st May 1991, travelling to Zimbabwe where he was offered Political Asylum.

➢ Milner (of St James and Cape Town), Alfred, 1st Viscount (1854-1925): He was a British Politician and Colonial Administrator. He established his reputation in Egypt and was appointed Governor of the Cape Colony and High Commissioner in South Africa (1897). There he became convinced that the British Position was endangered by the South African Republic (Transvaal), and he set about the political rationalisation of the region through the Boer Wars. He hoped to encourage sufficient English-speaking immigration to outnumber the Boers in South African dominion. He additionally became Governor of the Transvaal and Orange River Colony in 1901, but was forced to resign in 1905 as result of irregularities over Chinese labour he had introduced for the Rand Gold Mines. He was appointed Secretary of War (1916-19) and Colonial Secretary (1919-21), and died in Kent, England.

➢ Mobutu, Sese Seko Kuku Ngbendu Wa Za Banga Joseph Desire (1930- ): Zairian Solider and Politician, after army training and a period of study in Brussels, he joined the Belgian Force Publique in 1949. By 1956 he was Colonel; he joined Patrice Lumumba's Movement National Congolese in 1958 and became its Chief-of –Staff in 1960 at the time of Independence. The indecisiveness of the government in Leopoldville led him to take over the government to deal with the problem of Katanga's secession but he handed power back to Civilian rule within five months. After the 1963-5 Civil War, he intervened again this time permanently. He renamed the Country Zaire in place of the Belgian Congo and imposed a degree of stability in the country which had hitherto been unknown. He was backed by United States money and the power of the army his regime had become increasingly corrupt and unpopular?

➢ Mohamed, Murtala Ramal (1937-76): Nigerian Solider, he was a Muslim Hausa from Northern Nigeria, he trained at Sandhurst and the Royal School of Signals before returning to Nigeria and then serving in the UN Congo operation in 1960. He commanded the Nigerian 2nd Battalion at the start of the Biafra War and was made Federal Commissioner of Communications in 1974. When General Gowon was deposed in 1975, he became Head of State but was assassinated in an unsuccessful uprising on the 13th February 1976.

➢ Mohammed Ahmed (1884-85): The Mahdi, born in Dongola he was for a time in the Egyptian Civil Service, then a Salve Trader, and finally a relentless and successful rebel against Egyptian Rule in the Eastern Sudan. He made El Obeid his capital on 1883, and defeated Hicks Pasha and the Egyptian Army. In 1885 Khartoum was taken and General Gordon killed, he died later that year at Omdurman.

➢ Moi, Daniel Tarap (1924- ): Kenyan Politician, he was educated in local Schools he was a Primary School, and unqualified teacher (1946-56). He entered Legco in 1957 and then was elected for the Baringo Constituency which he represented 1963-78. He was Chairman of the Kenyan African Democratic Union (KADU) 1960-1, he was appointed Minister of Education in the coalition pre-Independence government of 1960-1 and after KADU had merged with the Kenyan African Union (KANU), he was appointed Minister of Home Affairs (1964-7). He became Vice-President of Kenya in 1967 and succeeded Jomo Kenyatta on the latter's death in 1978. He then shifted the ethnic balance of central politics away from the Kikuyu towards the Kalenjin people of Rift Valley. He cracked down hard on dissidents and opponents, reducing the already limited opportunities for meaningful political participation available to Kenyans. Despite an attempted Coup in August 1982 he has remained in power?

➢ Momoh, Joseph Saidu (1937- ): Sierra Leone Soldier and Politician, he was educated in Freetown and then Military School Academies in Ghana, Britain and Nigeria. He then was commissioned into the Sierra Leone Army in 1963. He was a Battalion Commander by 1968 and then was appointed Minister of State in 1975. When Siaka Stevens announced his retirement in 1985, Momoh, who had been hand picked to be Steven's successor he was endorsed by the countries only Political Party the People's Congress. Having won the election, he sought to distance himself from his predecessor's policies in an attempt to restrain corruption and reform the economy.

➢ Mondlane, Eduardo (1920-69): Mozambiquen Nationalist Leader, he was educated in Mission Schools, he furthered his education at Fort Hare College (South Africa) and the Lisbon University (Portugal).he developed into a respected Sociologist with research posts in the United States of America and within the United Nations. He returned to Mozambique in 1961 to form FRELIMO and then launched the Guerrilla War against the Portuguese Colonialism in 1964. He was murdered by a parcel bomb in Dar es Salaam.

➢ Motlana. Nthalo (1925- ): South African Doctor and Politician. He was educated at Kilnerton High School and Fort Hare College where he came into contact with the ANC (African National Congress) Youth League; he qualified as a Doctor at the University of Witwatersrand. Involved in establishing a network of ANC branches on the Witwatersrand. He was banned in 1953 for five years. By the mid-1970's he had become a leading figure in Soweto and played a major role in the 1976 Soweto Student Uprising. He helped establish the Soweto Committee of Ten, which developed into the Soweto Civil Association, of which he became Chairman. He was one of the few prominent figures to have lived in the Townships and has retained the respect of the ordinary citizens; he became an articulate spokesman for black interests in the 1980's while the ANC was still banned. ?

➢ Mubarak, Hosni (1928- ): Egyptian Politician, he was a Pilot in the Air Force and Flying Instructor who rose to become Commander of the Egyptian Air Force, He was appointed Vice President under Anwar Sadat from 1975 until Sadat's assassination in 1981. He was the only candidate for the Presidency after pledging to continue Sadat's domestic and International policies including firm treatment of Muslim extremists and the peace process with Israel. He was ousted out off power after 40 year legacy as President of Egypt by popular peoples uprising to his dictatorship. Normal Egyptians held vigil at Trobuk Square for 5 weeks demanding his resignation. He finally headed to popular demand and left the Army in charge in February 2011.

➤ Mugabe, Robert Gabriel (1924- ): Zimbabwean Nationalist leader and Politician. Educated in Catholic Mission Schools and Fort Hare College. He became a teacher in Southern Rhodesia, Northern Rhodesia and Ghana before returning to Southern Rhodesia in 1960 as Publicity Secretary to the National Democratic Party. He then became the Deputy Secretary-General of Zimbabwe African People's Union (ZAPU) in 1961 before being detained and then imprisoned; he then co-founded Zimbabwe African National Union in 1963. He was detained again (1964-74) during which period he replaced Ndabaningi Sithole as President of ZANU. He also qualified as a lawyer in prison. On his release in 1974, he went to Mozambique to oversee the Guerrilla War against the Ian Smith regime. He unified uncomfortably with Joshua Nkomo of ZAPU in the Patriotic Front, Mugabe essentially retained his independence and to the surprise of many led ZANU (PF) to a decisive victory in 1980 to become Zimbabwe's first Prime Minister. In December 1987 he became the Executive President but his radical views, both on the virtue of Socialism and his attempt to make Zimbabwe a One Party State of which he has failed. He still holds on to power with a coalition Government with the Movement for Democratic Change (MDC) led by Morgan Tswangirai. It has been rumoured that he has being diagnosed with terminal brain cancer.

➤ Museveni, Yoweri Kaguta (1944- ): Ugandan revolutionary Leader and Politician. He graduated at the Dar es Salaam University. He was the Assistant Secretary for Research in President Obote's Office until Idi Amins Coup of 1971. He returned to Dar es Salaam (Tanzania) as an Exile where he began the Front for National Salvation against Amin while teaching at the Cooperative College, Moshi. He led the attack on Mbarar, with Tanzanian troop's participation driving Amin from power. Museveni became Minster of Defence (1979-80) in the government of Yusof Lulu and Godfrey Binaisa but he fell out with Obote on the latter return to power. When the Tanzanian troops left in 1982 a virtual Civil War which ensued until 1986. Museveni's Forces prevailed and Obete once again fled the country. Museveni has since then attempted to follow a policy of National Reconciliation between the fighting factions.

➢ Muzorewa, Abel Tendekayi: (1925- ): Zimbabwean Cleric and Politician, he was educated in Methodist Schools in Southern Rhodesia (Zimbabwe) and at a Theological College in the United States of America, he was ordained in 1963 and he then became a Bishop of the United Methodist Church in Southern Rhodesia in 1968. He was the founding member and President of the African National Council in 1971; he failed to hold together the differing elements of the nationalist movement and chose the path of an internal settlement rather than Guerrilla War. After the ANC won the first Universal Suffrage election in 1979, he was Prime Minister of Zimbabwe-Rhodesia for a few months before the 1980 elections swept Robert Mugabe in power.

➢ Mwinyi, Ndugu Ali Hassan (1925- ): Tanzanian Politician, having trained as a Teacher, he taught in Zanzibar (1954-61) before going to the United Kingdom to further his studies. On his return he joined the Zanzibari Ministry of Education and then the Zanzibari State trading Corporation. In 1969 he became a Minister of State in the President Julius Nyerere and thereafter Minister of Health and Home Affairs, Minister of Natural Resources and Tourism, and then Minister of State in the Vice-Presidents Office. In April 1984 he was elected President of Zanzibar and in October 1985 he succeeded Nyerere as President of Tanzania. H e has since then tried to loosen the states control over the country's economy while retaining a faith in the Single Party the Chama Cha Mapinduzi (CCM)

➢ Nahhas, Mustafa al (1879-1965): Egyptian Politician, he was the leader of the WAFD in Egypt in 1923 and the Premier of Egypt in 1928, 1930 and 1950. In addition, al-Nahhas acted as regent for King Farouk in his early years and despite their being dismissed by Farouk in 1938, the WAFD were brought back in 1941 at the behest of the British. The damage done to the reputation of the WAFD by their cooperation with the British was irreparable. Although al-Nahhas became Premier again in 1950 at the WAFD's victory in the elections and despite his endeavours to regain credibility for the WAFD by giving the party an anti-British bias, they were again dismissed by Farouk in 1952. al-Nahhas then left the Political stage; he was charged but not tried for corruption. King Farouk was deposed by General Neguib on behalf of the Free Officers. The WAFD Party was dissolved in 1953.

➢ Nasser, Gamal Abd al (1918-70): Egyptian Politician, he was an Army Officer. He became dissatisfied with the corruption of the regime of King Farouk; he was involved in the Coup of 1952. He became Prime Minister (1954-6) and then President (1956-70), deposing his fellow Officer General Mohammed Nequib. During his term of Office he nationalised the Suez Canal, which led to the Israel's invasion of the Sinai, and the intervention of the Anglo-French Forces. He aimed to build a North African Arab Empire, and in 1858 created he created a federation with Syria, The United Arab Republic, from which Syria withdrew in 1961. After the Arab-Israeli Six Day War of 1976, heavy losses on the Arab side led to his resignation, but he was persuaded to stay on and then he eventually died while still in Office in Cairo in 1970.

➢ Nequib, Mohammed (1901-84): Egyptian Leader, as a General of the Army division in 1952 he carried out the Coup d'état in Cairo which banished King Farouk I and initiated the Egyptian Revolution. Taking first the Office of the Commander-In-Chief and the Prime Minister, he abolished the Monarchy in 1953 and became the First President of the Republic of Egypt. He was deposed in 1954 and was succeeded by Colonel Gama Abd al-Nasser.

➢ Neto, Antonio Agostinho (1922-79): Angolan Nationalist and Politician, he was the son of Methodist Missionary. He was educated in a Methodist School in Luanda before studying Medicine in Portugal Universities. He returned to Angola to work in the Colonial Medical Service and then he joined the MPLA. He was imprisoned several times between 1952062 but escaped from the Cape Verde Islands to Zaire where he soon became the President of the MPLA and the Leader of the Guerrilla War against the Portuguese Colonialism. His close ties with Fidel Castro gave him both Cuban and Soviet backing and this assistance enabled him to prevail in the Civil War which followed the Portuguese retreat from Angola. He became the first President of Angola in 1974, holding on to power until his death in?

➢ Nkomo, Joshua Mqabuko Nyongolo (1917- ): Zimbabwean Nationalist Leader and Politician. He was educated in Natal and at Fort Hare College, where he joined the ANC, he returned to Bulawayo as Social Worker and became General-Secretary of the Rhodesian Railway African Employees Association Congress in 1951, he became its President in 1957, leaving the country for Exile in 1959. When the ANC was banned he became President of its successor the National Democratic Party, but that too was banned. He then helped form the Zimbabwe African Peoples Union (ZAPU) of which he became its President. His non-confrontation tactics and tendency to spend time outside Rhodesia led to a more radical group breaking away to form the Zimbabwe African National Union (ZANU). ZANU and ZAPU developed with different international patrons and created separate Military Wings, which competed for the representation of the African opinion. They were persuaded to unite to form the Patriotic Front in 1976. ZAPU however was increasingly becoming an Ndebele Party and in the 1980 elections it won only 20 seats. Nkomo, who still saw himself as Father of Zimbabwe Nationalism, was disappointed to be offered Minster of Home Affairs, from which he was dismissed in 1981. Violence in Matabeleland encouraged him into a period of further exile, but he returned and agreed to integrate ZAPU into ZANU, a union ratified in April 1988. He became Vice-President of the New Party and was appointed one of the three senior members of the Parliament in the President's Office forming in-effect a super cabinet. ?.

➢ Nkrumah, Kwame (1909-71): Ghanaian Politician, he was educated in a Catholic Primary School and Achimota College, he then went to the USA and attended Lincoln and Pennsylvania University. He then went to London where he studied Law (1945-7). He became Co-Chairman of the Famous fifth Pan African Congress held in Manchester in 1945. He then returned to the Gold Coast as Secretary General of the United Gold Coast People's Party (CPP) in 1949. Imprisoned briefly he was elected to the Legco while in prison. He became leader of Government Business (1951), Prime Minister (1952-7) and he continued in the post on Independence until Ghana became a Republic in 1960 when he became the first President. He was a radical Pan- Africanist, for which he was widely admired throughout much of the Continent, he created considerable opposition within Ghana, most of which was repressed; ultimately, however, the Military intervened while he was abroad, symbolically on a visit to Beijing. He spent his life of Exile in Guinea where Seoul Toured gave him the status of Co-Head of State. He died in Bucharest?

➢ Nkumbula, Harry M (1916-83): Zambian Nationalist, he was educated in local Schools, he became a teacher before studying at Makerere College and then at the London School of Economics (1946-50). He was elected President of the Northern Rhodesian African National Congress (1951); he was then imprisoned briefly for his political activities. His support for a moderate Independence constitution cost him the support of Kaunda who left the ANC to form UNIP. He was a member of the pre-independence coalition government but was Leader of the Opposition during the first Republic elections. He was restricted for a while in 1970. When Zambia became a One Party State Republic, he joined UNIP in 1973 but remained outside politics in his last years.

➢ Nujoma, Sam Daniel (1929-?): Namibian Nationalist, he was educated at a Finnish Missionary School in Windhoek, he was a railway worker and a Clerk until entering Politics as the co-founder of the South West African People's Organisation (SWAPO). He went into exile in1960, he set up a provisional Headquarters in Dar es Salaam and led SWAPO's armed struggle from 1966 until 1989 when he returned to Namibia for the pre-independence elections which his Party won, he then became the first President Of Namibia in March 1990?

➢ Nyerere, Julius Kambarage (1922- ): Tanzanian Nationalist Leader and Politician. While working as a School Teacher, he became President of the Tanganyika African Association (1953). He left the profession to co-find the Tanganyika African National Union in 1954 of which he became President and led the Movement to Independence. After a brief spell as a nominated member of the Legco from which he resigned from the post to reorganise the Party and returned to Central Politics as President negotiating the Union of Tanganyika and Zanzibar in 1964. His idealism reflected the Arusha Declaration which dominated Tanzania public policy and the country's reputation abroad. He resigned the Presidency in 1985 but retained the Presidency of the Party until 1987.

➢ Obote, Apollo Milton (1924- ): Ugandan Politician who was educated in Mission School and at the Makerere College. He worked in Kenya (1950-5), before becoming a founder member of the Kenya African Union. He kept his Political links with his home Country were he was a member of the Uganda Congress (1952-60), being elected to the Legco in 1957. He helped form the Uganda People's Congress in 1960, he became it Leader and then he lead it as the opposition during the Kiwanuka Government of 1961-2. The 1962 elections resulted in a coalition with the Neo-Traditionalist Kabaka Yekka and he became Prime Minister. When fundamental differences between himself and the Kabaka which could not be mediated. He staged a Coup in 1966, deposing the Kabaka and establishing himself as Executive President. In 1971, however, his government was over thrown in a Military Coup, led by Idi Amin. He went into exile to Tanzanian and returned to Uganda with the Tanzania Army in 1979, regaining the Presidency after elections in 1980. He was overthrown again in a Military Coup; he went into exile again this time to Zambia.

➢ Odinga, Zaramogi Oginga Ajuma (1911-94): Kenyan Nationalist and Politician. He was educated at Alliance High School and Makerere College; he was a School Teacher when he became active in local politics. He was elected to Legco in 1957 and was Vice-President of KANU (1960-6), during which period he pressed unflinchingly for Independence, his apparent extremism being contrasted with the moderation of Mboya. He was appointed Minister of Home Affairs (1963-4) and then the Vice President (1964-6). At the Limuru Party Conference in 1966, Mboya managed to remove Odinga from positions of authority and he soon resigned to form the Kenya People's Union. He was re-elected on the KPU ticket in the general elections of 1966. He provided a Charismatic figure round which the dissidents to congregate. Consequently the party was soon banned and Odinga spent some of the next 25 years in and out of detention. ?

➢ Plaatje, Sol T (1876-1932): South African Journalist, Politician and Literary figure. One of the founders of the Black Nationalism, he first worked as a Post Office Messenger and then later as a Magistrates Court interpreter in Kimberly. He was in the town throughout the Siege during the Boer War and kept a lively diary of the events. After the War he founded and edited newspapers, wrote books including 'Native life in South Africa'. He translated Shakespeare into native tongue, Tswana, and was one of the founders of the South African Native Congress which later became the ANC.

➢ Pretorius, Andries Wilhelmus Jacobus (1819-1901): Afrikaner Leader, he was born at Graaff-Reinet, Cape Colony, he was a prosperous Farmer, who joined the Great Trek of 1835 into Natal, where he was chosen Commander-General. He later accepted British Rule, but after differences with the Governor he Trekked again this time across the Vaal. Eventually the British recognised the Transvaal Republic, and later the South African Republic, who's new Capital, was named Pretoria after him.

➢ Pretorius, Marthinus Wessel (1819-1901): Afrikaner Solider and Politician. The son of Andries Pretorius, he succeeded his father as Commander-General in 1853, and was elected President of South Africa Republic (1857-71), and of the Orange Free State (1859-63). He fought against the British again in 1877, until the Independence of the Republic was recognised (1881), and then he retired, and died at Potchefstroom.

➢ Ramaphosa, Matamela Cyril (1952- ): South African Trade Unionist, Politician and then Businessman. He became the Chairman of the all black South African Student Organisation (SASO) in 1974. After 11 months of detention in 1974-5, he became an Articled Clerk in Johannesburg and became active in the Black People's Convention (BPC); he was detained again in 1976. He graduated from the University of South Africa with a Laws Degree in 1981, he joined CUSA? as an adviser in its legal department. He became General-Secretary of the National Union of Mineworkers in 1982 and led into the first legal strike by mineworkers in September 1984. He amalgamated NUM? into COSATU (Congress of South African Trade Unions) and was elected Secretary-General of the African National Congress (ANC) in July 1991 at the Party's Conference held in Durban.

➢ Rhodes, Cecil John (1853-1902): A British who migrated to South Africa after studying in Oxford University. He entered the Cape House of Assembly, securing Bechuanaland as a protectorate (1885) and the Charter for the British South Africa Company (1889), whose territory was later to be named after him, as Rhodesia. In 1890 he became Prime Minister of the Cape Colony, but was forced to resign in 1896 because of complications arising from the Jameson Raid. He was a consipious figure during the Boer War of 1899-1902, when he organised the defences during the Siege of Kimberly. He died at Muizenberg, in the Cape Colony; in his will he left a Scholarship Fund for students to attend oxford and Rhodes University.

➤ Rodney, Walter (1942-80): Guyanese Historian and Politician, he was formerly Professor of the African History at the University of Dar es Salaam, Rodney provoked a riot when he was deported from Jamaica in 1968 for his supposed connections with Black Power. Although debarred from holding the History Chair of the University of Guyana, he returned to Guyana where he founded the Working People's Alliance which was antipathetic to the policies of the Burnham's Forbes Presidency of Guyana and the ruling People's National Congress. He wrote the book 'How Europe Underdeveloped Africa' in 1972. He was killed by a bomb under mysterious circumstances in Guyana.

➤ Sadat, Anwar el (1918-81): Egyptian Politician, he trained for the Army in Cairo, and in 1952 was member the coup which deposed King Farouk. After becoming President in 1970, he temporarily assumed the post of Prime Minister (1973-4), when as which he sought a settlement of the conflict with Israel. He met Menachem Begin the then Israeli Premier in Jerusalem in 1977 and at Camp David in the USA in 1978. Begin and Sadat were jointly awarded the Nobel Peace Prize. Following criticism by other Arab Statesmen and hard-line Muslims. He was assassinated while still in Office in Cairo by extremists.

➤ Sankara, Thomas (1950-87): Burkino Faso Solider and Politician, he joined the army in Ouagadougou in 1969 and attended the French Parachute Training Centre (1971-74) where he begun to acquire radical political ideas. As a Minister in Saye Zerbo's government he increasingly came to believe in the need for a genuinely popular revolution to expunge the consequences of French Colonialism. Leading a Coup in 1983, he became Prime Minister and Head of State. He introduced a wide range of progressive policies which made him enemies. Despite his great symbolic popularity among young radicals in and out of Burkina Faso on the 15th October 1987 he was shot dead during a coup led by his close associate Blaise Compaore.

➢ Savimbi, Jonas Malheiro (1934- ): Angolan Soldier and Nationalist Politician, he was educated in Angola and at Lausanne University, he returned to Zambia and became the Leader of the Popular Union of Angola, being Foreign Minister of the Angolan Government-In-Exile (1962-4). After period with the FNLA, he broke away to form UNITA and fought against the Portuguese until Independence. Unable to agree with the leaders of the MPLA and the FNLA, he continued the struggle against the MPLA from bases in the South of Angola supported by South Africa and the USA. A man of considerable charisma, he stood for a Democratic and Capitalist Angola, but his association with South Africa and USA made him a pariah in Third World Circles. However, the strength of his position and diplomatic bargaining by the USA led to a series of meeting designed to end the Civil War and remove the Cubans from Angola Agreement for a Ceasefire and Democratic elections was finally achieved in Estoril in 1991.

➢ Senghor, Leopold Sedar (1906- ): Senegalese Poet and Politician, he was educated in Roman Catholic Schools in Dakar, he went to the University of Paris and after graduation, taught in France (1935-9). He joined the French Army at the outbreak of War and was a prisoner (1940-2). A member of the Resistance (1942-4), he was a member of the French Assembly (1948-58), during which period ha was a University Lecturer. He was one of the founders of Presence Africaine in 1947 and wrote widely in that, and other Intellectual Magazines, establishing himself as a major Poet and the exponent of the philosophy of negritude. He formed the Union Progressive Senegalese in 1958 and as its Leader, became President of Senegal on the country's Independence in 1960. He retained cordial links with France and, although nominally a Socialist, espoused a Mixed Economy. In 1981 he retired from politics.

➢ Shagari, Alhaji Shebu Usman Aliyu (1925-) Nigerian Politician, he was educated in Northern Nigeria, he became a School Head Master before being elected as a member of the Federal Parliament (1954-8). He was Minister of Establishment (1960-2); Minister of Internal Affairs (1962-5) and Minister of Works (1965-6). After the 1966 Coup, he was made both State Commissioner for Education in Sokoto Province and Federal Commissioner for Economic Development and Reconstruction (1968-70) and then Commissioner for Finance (1971-5). He was a member of the Constituent Assembly which drew up the Constitution for the Second Republic and was the successful Presidential candidate for the National Party of Nigeria in 1979. He was President of Nigeria from 1979 until 1983, when he was overthrown in a Military Coup.

➤ Sisulu, Walter Max Ulyate (1912- ): South African Nationalist and Politician. After working as a Labourer in Johannesburg and then running his own Real Estate Agency, he joined the ANC in 1940, becoming Treasurer of the Programme of Action in 1949; he was elected Secretary-General of the ANC in the same year. He resigned his post because of Banning Orders, but continued to work underground. Sisulu was captured in 1963 and found guilty of treason, being sentenced in 1964 to life imprisonment. He was released in 1989 and took responsibility for the ANC's party's internal organisation after its legalisation in 1990.

➤ Sithole, Ndabaningi (1920- ): Zimbabwean Cleric and Politician, he worked as a teacher (1941-53) before going to the USA to study Theology (1953-6) and was Ordained a Congregational Minister in 1958. He wrote Africanlism in Nationalism in 1959, when he was also the President of the African Teachers Union. Sithole was Treasurer of the National Democratic Party in 1960 and after it was banned, he formed the Zimbabwe African People's Union (ZAPU) with Joshua Nkomo from which he split in 1963 and went on to form the Zimbabwe African National Union (ZANU). Imprisoned by the Rhodesian Front Government from 1964 to 1975, during which time the Leadership of ZANU was wrested from him by Robert Mugabe, he went into exile in Zambia in 1975 forming his own faction of ZANU the African National Council. He negotiated with Ian Smith and was a member of the Executive Council of the Transitional Government in Rhodesia-Zimbabwe (1978-80). Although he was elected to the first Post-Independence Parliament, he ceased thereafter to play any role in Politics.

➤ Slovo, Joe (1926- ): South African Nationalist, he was born in Lithuania, he immigrated to South Africa in 1935, where he worked as a clerk before volunteering for service in World War II. He joined the South African Communist Party (SACP) after the War. He qualified as Lawyer and defended many figures in political trials. He married Ruth First, daughter of the SACP Treasurer. He was a founding member of the Congress of Democrats in 1953. He was Charged in the Treason Trial of 1961, he nevertheless escaped the country in 1963 working for the ANC and SACP abroad. In 1985 he became Chief of Staff of the ANC Military Wing 'Umkhonto We Sizwe' but resigned from it to become the

Chairman of the SACP. He returned to South Africa after the legalisation of the SACP and was a major figure in the negotiations between the Nationalist parties of the ANC; PAC; IFP; BCM and the Government. He was appointed to?

➢ Smith, Ian Douglas (1919- ): Rhodesian Politician and Farmer. He was educated at Chaplin High School and Rhodes University. He served with the Royal Air force in World War II before returning to his farm. He was elected a member of the Southern Rhodesian Legislative Assembly in 1948 for the United Party and then, for the United Federal Party (UFP), to the Federal Parliament in 1953, becoming Chief Whip. He broke with the UFP, ostensibly on the question of Britain's failure to grant Independence to the White minority ruled state of Rhodesia. He helped found the Rhodesian Front (RF) in 1962; he replaced Winston Field as Leader of the (RF) after a putsch. He was elected Prime Minister from 1964 to 1978. He declared Unilateral Declaration of Independence (UDI) in 1965. He became a member of the Executive Council of the Transitional Government in Zimbabwe-Rhodesia which he initiated. He was elected to the Post-Independence Parliament in 1979. He retired to his farm and has been a vigorous opponent of Robert Mugabe and his government since?

➢ Smuts, Jan Christian (1870-1950): South African Republic General and Politician. He was educated at the University of Cambridge, he became a Lawyer. He fought in the Second Boer War (1899-1902), and entered the House of Assembly in 1907. He held several Cabinet Posts. He led campaigns against the Germans in South-West Africa (Namibia) and Tanganyika; he became a member of the Imperial War Cabinet in World War I and succeeded Louis Botha as Prime Minister (1919-24). He was a significant figure at Versailles and was instrumental in the founding of the League of Nations. As a Minister of Justice under Hertzog, his coalition with the Nationalist in 1934 produced the United Party with which he became the Premier of South Africa from 1939 to 1948.

➢ Sobukwe, Robert (1924-77): South African Nationalist Leader, he was educated at Mission Schools and at Fort Hare College, he was President of the Students Representative Council in 1949 and a was a member of the ANC Youth League. He was dismissed from his Teacher's post in 1952 because of his participation in the Defiance Campaign. He some how managed to still teach at Fort Hare College for seven years. He helped found the Pan-Africanist

Congress (PAC) in 1959 of which he was elected President. He was banned in 1960 and then imprisoned until 1969 when he was released, but restricted to Kimberley where he died in 1977.

➢ Steyn, Martinus Theunis (1857-1916): South African Politician, he was born in Winburg, Orange Free State, he was State President from 1868, and he joined it with the Transvaal in the Boer War (1889-1902). He promoted the Union of 1910, but later encouraged Boer extremists and their rebellion of 1914. His son Colin Fraser (1887-1959), mediated between General Botha and de Wet and was Minister of Justice in the Smuts Government (1939-45) and of labour (1945-8).

➢ Strijdom, Johannes Gerhardus (1893-1958): South African Politician, he was educated at Stellenbosch and Pretoria Universities, he was first a farmer and a Lawyer elected to parliament in 1929, and he became the major spokesman for the least flexible member of the National Party (NP) but was nonetheless made Minister of Lands and Irrigation when the NP came to power in 1948. He was chosen to succeed Malan as Leader and so became Prime Minister in 1954. He saw on of his cherished objectives achieved, namely Apartheid, but died before South Africa became a Republic.

➢ Suzman, Helen (1917- ): South African Politician, she was educated at Parktown Convent and Witwatersrand University, she lectured part-time at the university (1944-52) but became deeply concerned by right ward shift of the National Party. She joined the opposition the United Party and was elected to Parliament in 1953. She was closely involved with the South African Institute of Race Relations in the 1970's she was often a solitary voice against; Suzman earned the respect of opponents of apartheid and received the UN Human Rights Award in 1978. She retired from Parliament in 1989 after 36 years of service within the South African Parliament.

➢ Tambo, Oliver (1917-93): South African Nationalist Leader and Politician. The son of a Peasant Farmer, he went to Johannesburg to attend School set by the Community of The Resurrection where he came under the influence of Trevor Huddleston. After graduating from Fort Hare College, he embarked on teaching Diploma but was expelled for political activity. He joined the ANC Youth League in 1944, rising to be a member of the ANC Executive Committee

(1949), Secretary-General (1955) and Deputy President (1959). He then went into exile and became President of the ANC in exile from 1977. He returned to South Africa in 1989 as the Titular Leader of the Party, but gave up his position at the meeting of the Party in exile in 1990?

➢ Tutu, Desmond Mpilo (1931- ): South African Cleric, he was educated in Mission Schools and then at Pretoria Bantu Normal College, he studied at St Peter's and King's College, London. He was ordained as Deacon in the Anglican Church in 1960 and held a variety of Church Positions in England; South Africa and Lesotho, including lecturing at the Federal Theological Seminary in the Cape Province (1967-9), he also lectured at the Universities of Botswana; Lesotho; and Swaziland (1970-2). He returned from England to South Africa in 1975 as Dean of Johannesburg, from where went to be Bishop of Lesotho. As Secretary-General of the South African Council of Churches from 1978 to 1985, he spoke out strongly from the relative safety of his Church position against the extremes of Apartheid and was awarded the Nobel Peace Prize in 1984. He was elected Bishop of Johannesburg in 1986 and then Archbishop of Cape Town in the same year. He was a critic of the Apartheid System, he has also nonetheless also criticised violence in the Township of South Africa?

➢ Todd, Sir Reginald Stephen Garfield (1908-92): Rhodesian Politician. Born in New Zealand, he was educated there and also in South Africa. He came to Southern Rhodesia as a Missionary in 1934 he was elected to the Legislative Assembly (1946) and then to the Leadership of the United Rhodesia Party (1953) with which he became the Prime Minister in the same year. He was removed from the Leadership by an internal putsch because of his Liberalism and he helped form the overtly Liberal Central African Party in 1959. After the Party's failure in 1962, he returned to Farming but remained the spokesman for while Liberation in the Country, as a result of which he was restricted by the Rhodesian Front Government under Ian Smith (1965-6) and from (1972-6) he was became a close friend and ally of Joshua Nkomo, He supported Zapu in the 1980 Zimbabwean Impendence elections.

> Toure, Ahmed Sekou (1922-84): Guinean Politician, he was educated in Quran Schools and at Conakry (1936-40), he turned to Trade Union activity and attended the Confederation Ge`ne`rale des Travailleurs (CGT) congress in Paris in 1947, after which he was imprisoned for a brief period. He was founder member of the Reassemblement Democratique Africaine (RDA) in 1946 and became its Secretary-General in 1952, as well as Secretary-General of the Local (CGT) branch. He was a member of the Territorial Assembly from 1953, Mayor of Conarky in 1955 and then Deputy in the French National Assembly in 1956. In 1958 he organised an overwhelming 'none' vote to de Gaulle's referendum on self-government within a French Community. Guinea was granted its Independence immediately, the French removed as much of their possessions as possible. He was President from 1958 to 1984, and retained his uncompromisingly radical views of Domestic and Foreign Politics. He survived several attempts, supported by outside powers, to overthrow him. Soon after his death the military did take control?

> Tombalbaye, N'Garta Francois (1918-75): Chadian Politician, he was educated locally, he qualified as Teacher and practised before becoming a trades union organiser. He then helped organise the Reassemblement De`mocratique Africaine (RDA) in Chad in 1947 and was elected to the Territorial Assembly (1953). He rose to be Prime Minister in 1959 and then President on Chad's Independence in 1962. He remained in this position until the Military Coup of the 13th of April 1975, during which he was killed.

> Tolbert, William Richard (1913-80): Liberian Politician, he was educated at Liberia College in Monrovia. He was a Civil Servant (1935-43) before becoming a member of the House of Representatives for the True Whig Party 1943-51. Vice-President 1951-71; and then President of Liberia in 1971. He remained in this post until he was assassinated in a Military Coup on 12th April 1980.

> Tippu-Tib (1837-1905): He was one of the most powerful Traders and Plantation Owner of Zanzibar in the 19th Century. He created a personal empire in the eastern Congo region (Zaire) in the years before the Scramble for Africa. Tippu began to lead large and powerful trading caravans, financed by Indian Capitalists, into the interior of East Africa from the 1850's. Together with other Zanzibari Traders, he helped to establish networks of trade in Ivory

and Slaves throughout Eastern Zaire, became powerful in the markets there, and virtually ruled a large area for some 12 years. By the 1890's, he was backed in Zanzibar and owned seven plantations and some 10 000 slaves.

> Treurnicht, Andreis Petrus (1921- ): South African Politician, he studied at the Universities of Cape Town and Stellenbosch. He became a Minister in the Dutch Reform Church from 1946 until his election as National Party Representative in 1971. He was elected the Transvaal Leader of the Party in 1978, he held several Cabinet Posts under P.W Botha, gaining a reputation as an unreconstructed supporter of Apartheid. He opposed even Botha's partial Liberalisation of the regime and was forced to leave the Party; he left with 15 colleagues in 1982. He formed a new party the Conservative Party of South Africa which pressed for a return to Traditional Apartheid Values and the effective partitioning of the Country. The Party gained seats and votes, especially from the less well of Afrikaner. The Party took over from the Moderate Progressive Federal Party over the next decade?

> Tshombe, Moise Kapenda (1919-69): Congolese Politician, he was educated in Mission Schools, he was a Businessman who helped to found the Confederation des Associations du Katanga in 1957. When Belgium granted the Congo Independence in 1960, he declared the copper-rich province of Katanga Independent and became its President. On the request of Lumumba, UN Troops were called in to reintegrate the province and Tshombe was forced into exile in 1963; he returned again in 1964 supported by some of the mining interests and white settlers of Katanga. He was forced into exile again after Mobutu's 1966 Coup. Tshombe was kidnapped in 1967 and taken to Algeria where he died. He was a talented Conservative; he became the representation of Neo-Colonialism's ugly face in the mythology of African Nationalism throughout the Continent.

> Tsiranana, Philibert (1912- ): Madagascar Politician, he was educated on the Island and in France. He organised the Social Democratic Party, on whose ticket he was elected a member of the Representative Assembly in 1956, as well as the French National Assembly in 1957. He was Deputy President of Madagascar in 1958 and President in the following year. He remained in the post until being overthrown in a Military Coup in 1972.

➢ Tutu, Desmond Mpilo (1931- ): South African Cleric, he was educated in Mission Schools and at Pretoria Bantu Normal College. He studied at Saint Peters Theological College and at The King College London. He was ordained as Deacon in the Anglican Church in 1960 and held a variety of Church Positions in England; South Africa; Lesotho and Swaziland. He lectured at the Federal Theological Seminary in the Cape Province (1967-9), then at University Of Botswana, Lesotho and Swaziland (1970-2). He returned from England to South Africa in 1975 as Dean of Johannesburg, from where he went on to be Bishop of Lesotho. As the Secretary-General of the South African Council of Churches from 1978-1985, he spoke out strongly from the relative safety of his Church position against the extremes of Apartheid and was awarded the Nobel Peace Prize in 1984. He was elected Bishop of Johannesburg in 1985. He then appointed the Archbishop of Cape Town in 1986. He was public critic of the Apartheid System, he also nonetheless also criticised violence in the townships.

➢ Urabi Pasha (1839-1911): Egyptian Solider and Nationalist leader, he was an Officer in the Egyptian Army, he fought in the Egyptian-Ethiopian War of (1875-9) and took part in the Officers Revolt that deposed the Khedive, Ismail Pasha in 1879. He was then the leader of second rebellion against the New Khedive, Tewfif Pasha, in 1881, (the Urabi Revolt); this led to the setting up of a national government, in which he was made War Minister. The British intervened to protect their interest in the Suez Canal, and he was defeated as Tel el Kebir in 1882. He was sentenced to death but was exiled to Ceylon instead and was later pardoned in 1901.

➢ Usman dan Fadio (1754-1817): He was the Ruler of Hausaland, he was the leader of the Jihad or Holy War in Northern Nigeria, which resulted in the creation of a large Islamic Empire extending over some 180 000 square miles and 10 million people. A member of an Islamic Brotherhood in the small State of Gobir, Usman began to preach about 1775 calling for reforms in line with strict Islamic Doctrine. This was resisted by the Hausa Rulers. In 1804 he launched a Jihad against the ruling Hausa Aristocracy and founded his Capital at Sokoto. Many similar Jihads followed and Usman as Shehu or Chief of Sokoto was able to establish client Muslim Rulers over a vast area of Nigeria. This was an important part of the late 18th Century and early 19th Century movements to create African Islamic States which were to prove resistant to the advance of European Rule.

➢ Verwoerd, Hendrik Freusch (1901-66): South African Politician, he was born in Amsterdam Netherlands educated at Stellenbosch, where he became Professor of Applied Psychology (1927) and Sociology (1933), and edited the nationalist Die Transvaler (1938-1948) Elected Senator in 1948, he became Minister of Native Affairs (1980) and then Prime Minister (1958-66). His administration was marked by the highly controversial policy of Apartheid. The was an attempt on his life (1960), the establishment of the South African Republic in (1962) and later his assassination in Cape Town?

➢ Vieria, Jaao Bernardo (1939- ): Guinea-Bissau Politician, he joined the Party for the Independence of Portuguese Guinea and Cape Verde (PAIGC) in 1960, and in 1964 he became a member of the Political Bureau during the war for Independence from Portugal. After Independence in 1974, he served in the Government of Luiz Gabral but in 1980 he led the coup which disposed him. In 1984 Constitutional changes combined the roles of the Head of State and Head of Government making Vieria Executive President.

➢ Vorster, John Balthazar Johannes Vorster (1915-83): South African Politician, he was educated at Stellenbosch University, He later became a lawyer and was a Leader of the Extreme Afrikaner group, Ossewa Brandwag, in World War II as a result of the War. He was elected to Parliament for the National Party in 1953 and was Minster of Justice (1961-5) before becoming Prime Minister (1960-5) before becoming Prime Minister (1966-78) and for a brief moment the President of South Africa Republic. He was largely responsible for the imposition of the repressive Apartheid Laws and did not hesitate to employ state power to protect white interest. However, he was implicated in the Muldergate Scandal in which government funds had been misappropriated and was forced to resign.

➢ Welensky, Roland Roy (1907-92): Rhodesian Politician, he was born in Bulawayo Zimbabwe educated in local Schools and then started work on the Railways at the age of 14. He became a Leader of the Railway Workers Union in Northern Rhodesia in 1933, by which time he had also been Heavyweight Boxing Champion (1926-8). He was elected to the Northern Rhodesia Legco in 1938; he founded the Northern Rhodesia Labour Party in 1941 and was appointed Director of Manpower by the Governor. He became Chairman of the Unofficial Opposition in 1946. A strong supporter of the proposed Federation of the Rhodesia's and Nyasaland he was elected to its first Parliament. Welensky was appointed Minister of Transport and Development in 1953, to which he soon added the portfolios of Communications and Posts. He was promoted to Deputy Prime Minster in 1955; he succeeded Sir Godfrey Huggins Lord Malvern as Prime Minister in 1956, which he held until the Federations demise at the end of 1963. Although considered a doughty champion of White Rule, he was strongly opposed to Southern Rhodesia's UDI and tried unsuccessfully to return to politics as an opponent of Ian Smith, He eventually retired to a smallholding near Harare.

➤ Whitehead, Edgar (1905-71): Southern Rhodesian Politician, he was born in England, he immigrated to Southern Rhodesia in 1928 and after two years in the Civil Service, went into farming. He was elected to the Legislative Assembly in 1939 and after War service in the World War II; he became the country's High Commissioner in London (1945-6) before being called back as Minister of Finance (1946-53). After a further period of farming, he was asked to be the Central African Federation's Diplomatic Representative in the USA from where he was recalled again, this time to be Prime Minister his term of Office introduced served Liberalizing a move avowedly racist opposition of Ian Smith in the Rhodesian Front. He lost Office in the 1962 elections and retired, yet again to return to his farm.

➤ Wilson of Libya and Stowlagtofit, Henry Maitland, 1st Baron (1881-1964) as a  British Field Marshal he fought in the Boer War in South Africa and in the World war I, and at the outbreak of the World War II he was appointed Commander of The British Troops in Egypt. Having led the initial British advance in Libya (1940-1) and the unsuccessful Greek Campaign (1943) and Supreme Allied Commander in the Mediterranean Theatre (1944). Wilson headed the British Join Staff Mission in Washington (1945-7) and was raised to the peerage in 1946.

➤ Yameoyo, Maurice (1921- ): Burkina Faso Politician, he was educated in Upper Volta now Burkina Fuso. He was a Civil servant and Trade Unionist before turning to Politics and being elected to the Territorial Assembly in 1946. He was Vice President of the Upper Volta Section of the Conferation Francais du Tranvialleurs Chretiens and was active within the Reassemblement Democratique Africanine (RDA), The founder of the Movement De`mocratique

Voltaique (MDV), he was a Minister of Agriculture (1957-8), Minister of the Interior (1958) and then President (1958-66), before being toppled by a Military Coup on 4th January 1966 led by Lt-Col Sangoule Lamizana. He was imprisoned until 1970, when he went into exile in the Ivory Coast.

➢ Youla, Abbe Fulbert (1917-72): Congo Politician, he was educated in Catholic seminaries and Ordained as Priest in 1946, he became Mayor of Brazzaville in 1957 and was in turn Minister of Agriculture (1959-8), before being forced into exile in Spain as result of popular opposition within the Country.

➢ Zaghlul, Said (1837-1927): Egyptian Politician and Lawyer, effectively the founder of the Egyptian WAFD Party, he headed the campaign to change the political position of Egypt leading the delegation WAFD Egyptians who petitioned British for the end tom the Protectorate. This petition failed and as a result was banished to Malta (1919). Anti-British riots followed and he was released, later achieving the desired recognition of Independence for Egypt. After varying Fortunes, during the course of which he was once more arrested and banished Zaghlul eventually led his WAFD Party to success in Egypt's first elections. By 1924 Zaghlul had become Egypt's first Prime Minister; after a modern campaign conducted during the first WAFD Government meant, however, that despite the success once more of the WAFDist in the 1926 election, the British refused to accept Zaghlul as Prime Minister. He was allowed, though to become President of the Chamber, a cabinet containing six members of the WAFD, three Liberal and an Independent, with the Cabinet as a whole headed by the liberal Leader. Zaghlul, however, relinquished Office shortly afterwards.

➢ Zuma Jacob: He was born in Zululand He received no formal education. He has being engaged in politics an early age joined the ANC in 1959. He became an active member of the Umkhonto We Sizwe in 1962, following the banning of the ANC in 1961. He joined the South African Communist Party (SACP) in 1963 he was arrested with a group of 45 recruits near Zeerust in the Western Transvaal. He was convicted of conspiring to overthrow the Apartheid government he was sentenced to 10 years imprisonment of which he served at Robben Island with Nelson Mandela and other notable ANC leaders. After release, he was instrumental in the re-establishment of the ANC underground structures in Natal province. He left South Africa in 1975 and met Thabo Mbeki in

Swaziland and then proceeded to Mozambique, where he dealt with the arrival of thousands of exiles in the wake of the SOWETO uprising. He became a member of the ANC National Executive Committee in 1977. He also served as Deputy Chief Representative of the ANC in Mozambique a post he occupied until the signing of the Nkomati Accord between the Mozambican and Apartheid South African governments in 1984. He was appointed Chief Representative of the ANC, he also served on the ANC's Political and Military Council, and he was elected to the SACP's Politburo in April 1989. In January 1987 Zuma was again forced to leave a country this time Mozambique. He moved to the ANC Head Office in Lusaka Zambia where he was appointed Head of underground structures and shortly thereafter Chief of the Intelligence Department. His tenure there remains the subject of considerable controversy. Following the unbanning of the ANC in February 1990, he was one of the first ANC Leaders to return to South Africa to begin the process of negotiations. In 1990 he was elected Chairperson of the ANC for Southern Natal region and took a leading role in fighting political violence in the region between member of the Ikatha Freedom Party and the ANC. He was elected the Deputy Secretary General of the ANC and in January 1994 he was nominated as the ANC candidate for Premiership of KwaZulu Natal. After the 1994 general elections, with the ANC becoming the governing party but having lost KwaZulu Natal to the IFP, he was appointed as Member of the Executive Committee (MEC) of Economics Affairs and Tourism for the KwaZulu Natal provincial government. After stepping aside to allow Thabo Mbeki to run unopposed for Deputy Presidency. In December 1994 he was elected National Chairperson of the ANC and Chairperson of the ANC in KwaZulu Natal. He was elected Deputy President of the ANC at the National Conference held in December 1997 and consequently Executive Deputy President of South Africa in June 1999. During this time, he also worked in Kampala, Uganda as a facilitator of the Burundi peace process along with Ugandan President Yoweri Museveni. On 14th June 2005 he was expelled from his post Deputy President due to corruption and fraud related to the $5 billion weapons acquisition deal by the South African government in 1999. In terms of party tradition as Deputy President of the ANC, Zuma was already in line to succeed Mbeki. The party structures held their nominations conference in October and November 2007, where Zuma appeared favourite for the post of ANC President, and by implication the President of South Africa in 2009. Zuma was elected President of the ANC on 18th December

2007 with 2329 votes beating the second term and South African President Thabo Mbeki with 1505 votes. On 28th December 2007, the National prosecuting Authority served Zuma an Indictment to stand trail in the High court on various counts of racketeering, money laundering, corruption and fraud. In September 2008 the ANC ruled Thabo Mbeki unfit to rule a country thus ending his parliamentary support and forced him to resign from the country's Presidency. It was announced that the party's Deputy President Kgalema Motlante would become caretaker President until 2009 general elections, after which Zuma would become President, he won the election on 6 May 2009 and was sworn in as President of South Africa on 9th May 2009.

## PART FOUR: UNITED COUNTRIES OF AFRICA (UCA)

**A PROPOSAL FOR AFRICAN DEMOCRACY:** by Kwame Nkrumah
"That was the message then. That is the message now. Africa Unification Now! The importance of the message to the success of Africa has compelled me to make a proposal to the people of Ghana and Africa. It is to enable the people of Africa to obtain the benefits of African Unification comfortably, easily and smoothly. I propose to the people of Ghana and Africa. That? The Political Kingdom of Africa The United Africa be founded and governed by the tenets and philosophy of the African Democracy. The Proposal of African Democracy is based on my strong belief that the attainment of the benefits of African Unification is greatly dependent on the creation of the right form of unification in Africa. I believe strongly that the right form of African Unification is greatly dependent on The Federation of Modern African States and Traditional African states (The ethnic nations of Africa before the partition of Africa). Given Africa's? unique social-political structure, the unity of African states and African Ethnic Groups is the unification model suitable for Ghana and Africa. Therefore, I propose United Africa to replace the fragmented and disunited geopolitical entities in Africa today. I propose the Federation of African States and African Ethnic Groups, one united African Country founded on and governed by African Democracy. African Democracy is simply the meaningful separation of geopolitical powers and the meaningful separation of institutional political powers all guided by African centric political ideology. African Democracy is essential to obtaining? The all else shall be added unto to you? Which is the benefit of the African Unification, and which is peace for all African, prosperity for all Africans and prestige for all Africans. I believe that, the proposed African Democracy, is the most appropriate form of African Unification because of Africa?s unique social and geopolitical structure and will be most acceptable to most Africans. The right democracy for Africa? The African Democracy consist of the right political structure, the right political systems and the right political ideology".
The Way forward from Colonization; Nationalisation; Tribelisation and Regionalisation is by forming The Untied Countries of Africa in the same model as the European Union. The time has now come for all Africans that is every black man and woman in the world to set up Democratic dispension in each African Country we can forgive but must never forget Slavery, learning from our former Liberation Leaders and their Movements that freed us from Colonialism and led us to Independence. Its now time for Africans to have elected Democratic Leaders who will lead each different African Country into Democratic Governance in each

African Country in accordance to the Democratic Manuel of the United Nations. The UCA will take over the current functions of the Organisation of African Unity (OUA) we need to look into the fiscal structure of the European Union and simulate the same formula in to the formation of the Untied Countries of Africa (UCA). We need to combine our Gross Domestic Product (GDP) in-order to form one currency which I suggest can be called the Corrie as in the Corrie shell.

**THE ECONOMIC AND POLITICAL UNION OF THE 53 COUNTRIES THE UNITED COUNTRIES OF AFRICA (UCA):** should operate through a hybrid system of supranational Independent institutions and intergovernmental made decisions negotiated by the member states. The UCA will implement the following institutions which are the **AFRICAN COMMISSION** which will be the Executive Body of the African Union. The body is responsible for proposing Legislation, implementing decisions, upholding the Unions treaties and the day-to-day running of the Union. The African Union Commission will operate as a Cabinet government with 53 commissioners. One of the 53 States will be Commission President appointed by the UCA Council. The Council will then appoint the other Commissioners in agreement with the nominated President and then the 53 Commissioners as a single body are subject to a vote of approval by the Parliament. The African Commission institution will include the administrative body of civil servants who will be spilt into two departments the Directorates-General and Services.

**THE AFRICAN COUNCIL:** The institution of the council of Ministers representing their governments, the other legislative body will be the African Parliament. The Council/Parliament will be composed of the 53 national ministers. The Presidency of the Council will rotate every six months between the governments of the UCA member states. The African Council will refer to the regular meeting of the Head of State or of government in the UCA, responsible for the defining the general direction and the priories of the union. It will comprise of the heads of State from each country in the UCA along with its President of the Commission. The High Representative takes part in its meeting which will be chaired by it President,

**THE AFRICAN COURT OF JUSTICE:** The institution of the UCA which will encompass the whole African Judiciary which will be seated some where in the middle of Africa. It will be split into the three sub courts, The African court of Justice; The General Court and the Civil Service Tribunal.

**THE AFRICAN CENTRAL BANK (ACB):** the institution of the UCA which will administer the monetary policy of the 53 states. It is thus going to be on of the Worlds most important Central Banks

**THE AFRICAN PARLIAMENT:** It will be made up of the directly elected parliamentary candidates who make the institution of the UCA; together with the Council of the African Union it will form the bicameral legislative branch of the African Union,

**CITIZENSHIP OF THE UNITED COUNTRIES OF AFRICA** is hereby established, every person holding the nationality of a member State shall be a citizen of the Union. Citizenship of the Union shall be additional to and not replace national citizenship. All nationals of member states will be citizens of the Union. It is for each member state, having due regards to Community Law.

**THE AFRICAN MARKET:** the African union UCA will have to develop a single market through a standardised system of Laws which will apply in all members' states including the abolition of passport controls within African Boarders. It will ensure the free movement of people, goods, and services and maintain common policies on trade, agriculture, fishery and regional development. A monetary union the AfriZone (Corrie) will be established. The United Countries of Africa through the common foreign and Security Policy the Union will develop a limited role in the external relations and defence.

Made in the USA
Las Vegas, NV
18 April 2021